Winning NLRB Elections

Avoiding Unionization Through Preventive Employee Relations Programs

Fourth Edition

Jackson Lewis

CCH INCORPORATED
Chicago

"The National Labor Relations Act proceeds on the understanding that the employer has a right commencing on the date of hire to convince its employees that union representation is not in their interest."

Report by the House Education and Labor Committee on the Labor Law Reform Bill of 1977

"The expressing of any views, argument, or opinion, or the dissemination thereof, whether in written, printed, graphic, or visual form, shall not constitute or be evidence of an unfair labor practice under any of the provisions of this Act, if such expression contains no threat of reprisal or force or promise of benefit."

Section 8(c), National Labor Relations Act

FOREWORD

Winning NLRB Elections continues to be the best and most comprehensive management publication on how to establish and maintain a union-free workplace.

The original version of the book was written in 1972 by Louis Jackson and Robert Lewis, the founding partners of Jackson Lewis. Until then, there was a dearth of literature on how an employer could lawfully and appropriately deal with union organizing. The Jackson Lewis book filled this need.

By 1979, union organizing had increased and the law had changed. That year, a revised edition was written by Mr. Lewis and his partner, William A. Krupman. In 1991, a third edition was published. During the past six years significant changes in the law and procedures have required further revision and updating.

As with previous editions, the 1997 edition of *Winning NLRB Elections* is based on the combined experience of Jackson Lewis attorneys who have participated in over 3,000 NLRB election proceedings and who regularly advise clients and train managers on their legal rights and responsibilities concerning organizing campaigns and preventive programs.

We recommend this unique book as the most comprehensive proactive publication on positive employee relations, preventive programs and success in handling NLRB elections. A review of the first edition, which is as timely today as it was 25 years ago, follows.

CCH INCORPORATED

REVIEW OF FIRST EDITION

CURRENT LITERATURE

In the Labor Field

Winning NLRB Elections: Management Strategy and Preventive Programs. Louis Jackson and Robert Lewis. Practising Law Institute. One Volume. 357 pages. **Reviewed by Joseph Brandschain**—Head, Labor Law Department (retired), Wolf, Block, Schorr & Solis-Cohen, Philadelphia. Labor arbitrator.

Lou Jackson and his partner, Bob Lewis, have dared to write a daring book and Practising Law Institute has dared to publish "Winning NLRB Elections: Management Strategy and Preventive Programs," a labor law, labor relations treatise, the thrust of which has until now been off limits, a "no-no" for writers in this field. Until this publication, there has been something of an unnecessary taboo on the discussion of the subject of employer activities against a union organization to defend a campaign directed toward his employees; it has been treated mostly by guarded, furtive discussion, as if the subject fell short of respectability, even in management circles.

These attitudes were, no doubt, residual feelings from Wagner Act days when the National Labor Relations Board administered the Act in a way designed to deter employers from engaging in any act or voicing almost any thought in opposition to a union drive against his employees. Even though the Board began to shift away from this stance and to recognize employer free speech rights in the early '40's, to which later the Taft-Hartley Amendments of 1947 gave legislative validity, there has nevertheless persisted the feeling that employer activity in stating his case, although quite legal if he stayed within the circumscribed limits as they continue to be defined by the Board and Court proscriptions against promises and threats, was "not (entirely) cricket." Thus, while the period since Taft-Hartley has seen a proliferation of such activity by employers abetted by management lawyers and labor relations consultants, people still did not rush into print to delineate techniques for drives to thwart union organizing drives.

The book is a frank and unabashed, direct, yet restrained primer, without venom or rancor, for employers and their lawyers, who conclude that the employer's best economic and operating interests lie in keeping a workforce union-free.

The aim and techniques of the book are based on the thesis that the statement of the purpose in the preamble to the NLRA to grant workers and unions the right to organize, does not bar the employer's right to oppose such organization or place any moral opprobrium upon his activities so long as he does not transgress legal limitations.

If Steve Schlossberg, able and highly respected counsel for the Auto Workers Union, can write a book on "How to Organize," the authors suggest that they may write one on how to oppose organization. They do not belabor this point, except in passing, by asserting that the role and restrictions upon supervisors in a unionized plant are more difficult as a result of often being hamstrung by shop stewards in dealing with employees ... and very near the end of the book by stating that "... an employer who has a union has a partner in his business ... Every year or two there will be demands and crises. With some unions, there will be no further contact until the next round of negotiations. With others, the turmoil will be constant. Grievances and confrontations will be his daily diet."

What the book suggests, without spelling it out in so many words, is that in a capitalistic, free enterprise economy, an employer should have another choice or alternative to this mode of carrying on his business. Practising Law Institute's imprimatur on the book's publication, if it does not underwrite this thesis, at least underwrites the authors' and employers' rights of free speech and employees' rights to be informed. The book stresses these employee rights at length by analyzing the need for the employee to scrutinize union activities, the record of the particular union organizing a plant and the employer's record vis-a-vis his employees.

Moreover, the book emphasizes an approach based on fair dealing with employees, and that in communicating with employees a "straight from the shoulder" presentation is best. It is not a time for subtlety ..."

The book starts with prophylactic steps which an employer should take before the union knocks on his door or sends in a request for representation. It then traces in great detail the steps to be taken in an employer counter campaign to combat a union organizing campaign. Sometimes, it seems that the steps are too detailed and too repetitive, but who can quarrel with success; Jackson and Lewis have a notable record of high expertise and wide experience (Jackson for over three decades) in management representation in all phases of labor relations, including significant success in National Labor Relations Board election proceedings. Moreover, no doubt the art of teaching requires repetition and emphasis, and the aim here is to instruct, so that it is probably not valid to assume that something said or written once has sunk in, especially when, by and large, the employer is dealing with a not highly educated "student body."

The book is a very good do-it-yourself handbook of how an employer should behave both before and when he has met with an organizational drive. However, despite the detailed campaign material it outlines and illustrates, and despite the frank revelation of a "million dollars worth" of the authors' professional "secrets" in this field, it is doubtful whether it ought to be used without the guidance of experienced professionals. While the book charts and steers a careful course to avoid groundings on the reefs of unfair labor practice charges, it would be unwise to attempt to follow it without a pilot who can keep the employer's craft safely in mid-channel.

The book also outlines with meticulous precision, step by step and in fine detail, the procedures in NLRB representation and election proceedings.

And, as a final touch, just to prove that it is not a labor-baiting, unreconstructed, anti-labor diatribe, the authors conclude that as to an employer who has lost an election:

"He will learn to live with his union, as do the employers of some 19 million employees."

Labor Law Journal, November 1972, pp. 707-708

ACKNOWLEDGMENTS

The partners of Jackson Lewis express their appreciation to Louis Jackson, Robert Lewis, William A. Krupman, Margaret R. Bryant and Roger S. Kaplan for their efforts in rewriting this book.

The assistance of the following partners who contributed to this edition is also gratefully acknowledged: Christopher C. Antone, Howard M. Bloom, Robert M. Cassel, G. Harrison Darby, Patrick Egan, Robert J. Giovannetti, Steven S. Goodman, Jeffrey M. Mintz, Martin F. Payson, Andrew A. Peterson, Michael N. Petkovich, Thomas P. Piekara, James A. Prozzi, Philip B. Rosen, Lewis H. Silverman, Lawrence H. Stone and Patrick L. Vaccaro. The research and writing assistance of Matthew J. Camardella and the secretarial skills of Jean Nobile were invaluable.

ABOUT THE FIRM AND CCH

JACKSON LEWIS is a national labor and employment law firm representing management exclusively. It has offices in Atlanta, Boston, Chicago, Dallas, Greenville, South Carolina, Hartford, Connecticut, Larkspur, California, Los Angeles, Miami, Minneapolis, Morristown, New Jersey, New York City, Orlando, Pittsburgh, San Francisco, Stamford, Connecticut, Washington, D.C., White Plains, New York, and Woodbury, Long Island. Jackson Lewis is one of the largest law firms in the country engaged exclusively in this specialty and represents a broad cross section of clients, large and small, in every industry and in every state.

Jackson Lewis was the first firm to actively practice preventive labor and employment law. From its beginning in 1958 the firm has stressed that the education of management is the key to avoiding legal problems. This preventive approach continues to be the foundation of its practice and a key motivating factor in writing this book, now in its fourth edition.

CCH INCORPORATED is a leading provider of human resources, business law and tax information and software. Since 1913, it has provided reference and productivity tools to help human resources and business professionals be proactive in developing effective policies and procedures while complying with federal, state and local laws. CCH is a wholly owned subsidiary of Wolters Kluwer, N.V.

TABLE OF CONTENTS

PART I

PREVENTION AS PRELUDE

PART II

THE EARLY STAGES

PART III

WINNING THE ELECTION

LIST OF ILLUSTRATIONS

PREFACE TO FOURTH EDITION

The purpose of this book is to provide guidance to human resources professionals, corporate counsel, private practitioners, business owners, supervisors, labor relations teachers, and students on how a company can remain union-free. The concept is more than theoretical. Faced with the renewed challenge of extensive union organizing, employers have rededicated themselves to implementing positive employee relations practices that will foster a union-free workplace.

Why Be Union-Free?

There are five stakeholders in a corporate enterprise: (1) management and supervisors; (2) the employees; (3) the investors, shareholders and owners; (4) the communities in which the company operates and the employees reside; and (5) the customers. Each of them could be seriously affected if a union succeeds in organizing a workplace and influencing daily working relationships.

Management

With a union, management may be impeded in its relationship with its employees. In responding to individual concerns, communications must flow through union functionaries. The workplace may become polarized and confrontational, with endless hours spent in trying to define *who's* right rather than *what's* right. Complaints and grievances may consume hours of managerial time diverted from production, sales, and other enterprise pursuits.

Employees

With a union, employees may experience an entirely different, and often negative, working relationship. A union often creates impediments to direct communication between employees and supervisors in the guise of shop stewards and business representatives. In most cases, employees will incur financial obligations including union-imposed dues and initiation fees. They may fall prey to union politics, union-imposed discipline, the uncertainty of negotiations, and the potential of strikes.

Owners

Corporate investors, who have put their personal resources at risk in the expectation of a reasonable return on investment, may find it more profitable to deploy their assets elsewhere. Even if this does not occur, the union may slow the company's ability to respond to customer demands, thereby inhibiting a maximization of profits.

Community

The community benefits significantly when the company creates jobs, employees spend their incomes at local businesses, the tax base increases, and civic and charitable interests are supported. But, as communities like Peoria and Decatur, Illinois learned in the Caterpillar strike, the very fabric of the social structure can be torn apart with enduring animosity and distrust. Numerous other communities have had similar experiences—never to be forgotten.

Customers

Finally, customer satisfaction may decline if the union threatens the reliability and quality of the products and services and drives up costs and prices. The biggest threat to customer loyalty is the strike. Consumers often are unwilling to "wait out" an economic struggle between employer and union, largely because many other companies can provide the same goods or services. Ultimately, the loss of customers is detrimental to the other stakeholders.

Thus, the answer to the question "Why be union-free?" is self-evident. A company can be managed more efficiently if it can communicate directly with its employees and be free to implement flexible workplace policies. By following the positive employee practices outlined in this book, management will be able to make a convincing case for staying union-free.

Unionization in 1997 and Beyond

The AFL-CIO is publicly proclaiming a crusade to organize millions of workers and has allocated $30 million for this purpose, starting in 1997. John J. Sweeney, the labor federation's president, has called for "a national organizing resurgence" and has pledged "to organize every working woman and man who needs a better deal." Indeed, during the first half of 1997 the AFL-CIO held thirteen regional conferences at which it discussed strategic organizing strategies, new organizing tactics, mobilizing members to support organizing campaigns, and building community support for organizing.

The increasing number of working women is a promising source of new union members. By the year 2000, the number of women in the work force is projected to surpass the number of men. Studies also show that when women constitute a majority of a voting group, unions win more than half of representation elections. If this trend continues, union membership is almost certain to increase. Realizing this, unions are training female organizers who are able to speak convincingly about "women's issues," such as child care, medical care, parental leave, equal pay for equal work, sex discrimination, and safety and health.

Preventive Strategies for Avoiding Outside Interference

Anticipating this new wave of organizing, the fourth edition of this book takes a fresh look at preventive strategies that have proven effective in maintaining a union-free status.

An important preventive strategy gaining acceptance and popularity is alternative dispute resolution, or ADR, which offers employees options to resolve problems internally rather than resorting to litigation, unions, or self help. Another strategy is employee participation programs which encourage employees to talk about their jobs and concerns that influence their worklife.

Employees have become aware of the right to engage in activity with other employees for mutual aid and protection, with or without union involvement. Increasingly, workers are filing unfair labor practice charges against employers who interfere with this right. A chapter discussing concerted activity addresses this development.

How This Edition Is Organized

A word about the format: This book is separated into three parts. Part I discusses the union-free employer and key aspects of a positive employee relations program. Part II deals with employee self-help through protected concerted activities, how unions organize and employer responses. Part III analyzes the procedures for holding a National Labor Relations Board election and contains a day-by-day campaign calendar outlining management strategies the month prior to the election.

Augmenting the discussion of strategies, tactics, and procedures are extensive illustrations of handouts, letters, speeches, posters, and other material proven effective in actual campaigns, allowing the reader to experience a union organizing campaign from its early warning signs to an actual Labor Board election. In non-technical language, the reader is guided through the maze of rules and procedures involved in the election process toward the goal of victory. First-hand experiences of veteran labor relations attorneys demonstrate how the employer can best position itself to avoid or win an election.

One technical note: Extensive case citations have been avoided; where citations are used, they include only the name of the case, the year of decision, and the decisionmaker. Labor Board decisions bear only the name of the employer and the date. The identity of a court is shown by customary designation. Complete citations to Board and court decisions (through March 1997) are included in the alphabetical table of cases at the back of the book. A Glossary of Labor Terms is included as an Appendix.

The Challenge

Guided by the principles of an effective employee relations program, as outlined in the book, the union-free employer can pursue its business objectives and, when confronted with the threat of unionization, successfully meet the challenge.

Preventing unionization is not a do-it-yourself project. Timely legal advice is essential; a cooperative effort between employer and counsel is imperative. We begin with an overview of the law.

PART I

PREVENTION AS
PRELUDE

CHAPTER I

AN OVERVIEW OF THE LAW

The law embodying the basic labor-management relations policy of the United States is the National Labor Relations Act ("NLRA" or "Act"). Enacted in 1935, the NLRA (then known as the Wagner Act) was amended in 1947 by the Labor Management Relations Act (Taft-Hartley Act) and in 1959 by the Labor Management Reporting and Disclosure Act (Landrum-Griffin Act).

The Act covers all businesses whose materials, products, or services cross state lines and those which affect other businesses engaged in such activities. (Businesses not covered by the Act may be governed by state and local laws.)

The purpose of the Act is to encourage the practice and procedure of collective bargaining by protecting the right of employees to exercise freedom of association, self-organization, and designation of representatives of their own choosing. It also protects their right to refrain from engaging in such activities.

The Act authorized the creation of the National Labor Relations Board to administer and enforce the law. The Board [1] is authorized to issue rules and regulations and to establish procedures to carry out its statutory functions. It has five members, and its principal office is in Washington, D.C. Board members are appointed by the President, with approval of the Senate, and serve five-year terms. The duties of the Board are two-fold: (1) to conduct secret ballot elections among employees to determine whether they desire representation by a labor organi-

---

[1] When used in this chapter, the term "the Board" or "Labor Board" refers to the five members in Washington who adjudicate unfair labor practice and representation cases; the reference to "the NLRB" is to the agency as a whole. Elsewhere, the terms are used interchangeably.

zation, and (2) to prevent and remedy unfair labor practices. The Board appoints an Executive Secretary to carry out its duties.

A General Counsel is appointed by the President, with the approval of the Senate, and serves for a term of four years. He or she supervises the regional directors and employees in the regional offices and all attorneys employed by the Board except Board members' staff attorneys. By statute, the General Counsel has final authority (through the regional directors) to investigate unfair labor practice charges, to issue complaints, and to prosecute them.

The law prohibits specific conduct by employers and labor organizations as unfair labor practices. In general, section 8(a) of the Act makes it unlawful for an employer to: interfere with, restrain, or coerce employees in exercising their right of self-organization; dominate or interfere with the formation or administration of a labor organization; encourage or discourage membership in a labor organization; discriminate against an employee because he filed charges or gave testimony; or refuse to bargain collectively with the majority representative of its employees.

Union unfair labor practices are defined in section 8(b) of the Act. In general, it is unlawful for a labor organization to: restrain employees in the exercise of their rights under the Act; coerce an employer in the selection of a bargaining representative; attempt to cause an employer to discriminate against an employee because of his non-membership in a union; refuse to bargain in good faith; or engage in a secondary boycott.

Section 9 of the Act governs the procedure for the selection of employee representatives. It provides for several different types of elections: a "representation" election to determine the majority status of a labor organization; a "decertification" election to determine whether a currently certified or recognized union still represents a majority of the employees; and a "deauthorization" election to determine whether a union should continue to have the authority to enforce a union-shop agreement compelling the payment of dues as a condition of employment.

The procedures for holding these different types of elections are described in the Board's rules and regulations and operations manuals. The most common election is to determine whether a union will become the employees' representative. An election petition may be filed by a union if supported by at least 30% of the employees in a unit appropriate for bargaining. Signed authorization cards are evidence of this support. To win an election the union must receive a majority vote of the employees who cast ballots in the bargaining unit.

There are thousands of Board decisions interpreting sections 8 and 9 of the Act, many of which are referred to throughout this book.

CHAPTER II

THE UNION-FREE EMPLOYER

Why are some employers targets of union organizing activity while others enjoy relative freedom from union intrusion? The answer almost always lies in the philosophy and design of an employer's employee relations program.

At the outset, a company must examine its attitude toward unions. Some employers assume unionization is inevitable. Statistics, however, reveal the contrary: unions lose half of the elections in which they participate. Furthermore, unions report a combined membership of 16 million. Out of a total work force of 110 million, unions represent only 15%. After many years of organizing, this does not equate with inevitability.

The employer whose objective is to operate without a union has an excellent chance of doing so, but it requires a commitment to practice preventive employee relations. This means developing an employee relations program designed to build morale and loyalty through open communications with its employees. Such a program must be initiated long before any signs of union organizing activity occur and must be maintained with abiding dedication.

The experienced union-free employer knows that an employee's loyalty cannot be purchased merely with money and benefits. It must be nurtured by a commitment to caring about the employee's well-being. Workers want to be treated with consideration and thoughtfulness. Listening to employee concerns and attending to their needs is the best way to earn and maintain employee loyalty and confidence.

Two-way communications is the keystone of a successful employee relations program. Other elements include:

- An avenue for effective resolution of employee problems;

- An opportunity for personal growth and job advancement;

- Interesting work;

- Recognition of and incentive for good work performance;

- Respect for self-esteem and needs of the individual;

- Consistent administration of company policies and disciplinary procedures;

- A safe and healthy work environment;

- Written, up-to-date personnel policies; and

- Wages and benefits comparable to similarly situated employees in the industry or the community.

The challenge for the union-free employer is to combine these elements into a comprehensive preventive employee relations program.

CHAPTER III

DEVELOPING A PREVENTIVE EMPLOYEE RELATIONS PROGRAM

A preventive employee relations program is one designed to prevent employment-related disputes from arising. It is the application of the adage "an ounce of prevention is worth a pound of cure." A preventive program helps management achieve lower labor costs through greater employee productivity, reduces absenteeism and turnover, and increases employee morale. Employees benefit too. Working for a profitable business, they enjoy steady, secure employment and regular improvement in their wages and benefits.

To develop a preventive employee relations program, the employer should first conduct an in-depth study of its current personnel policies and labor related experiences—a preventive audit.

THE PREVENTIVE AUDIT

A detailed preventive audit includes obtaining information concerning the following subjects:

- Personnel administration

    Director of human resources and staff

    Functions performed

    Professional quality

- Supervisory staff

    Recruitment and training of supervisors

    Extent of involvement in personnel functions

- Composition of non-supervisory staff

By job classification

By equal employment opportunity categories
- The employment process

  Sources of labor

  Employment forms—requisitions, employment applications

  Job specifications

  Interviewing guides

  Tests and their validation

  Reference checks

  Applicant files—conditional hiring

  Physical examination

  Final approval

  Orientation of the new employee

  Introductory period and its use

  Equal employment opportunity policies

  Affirmative action program
- Transfers, promotions, upgrading, and demotion

  General policy, seniority, merit consideration

  Compensation considerations

  Job bidding procedures
- Termination of employment

  Review and appeals of discharge cases

  Exit interviewing and use of the results

  Turnover statistics—analysis of reasons and use of the analysis
- Comprehensive wage chart

  Rates for all jobs and employee classifications

  Compliance with equal opportunity employment laws
- Job evaluation and wage progression system

  Incentive plans

  Piece work

Day rate

Commissions

Production standards

Time study

● Wage and salary administration

History of general wage increases

Merit reviews

Cost of living adjustments

Overtime premium pay—daily, weekly, Saturday, Sunday

Overtime distribution procedure

Shifts and shift differentials

Pay for holidays worked

Reporting and call-in pay, pay for time lost due to weather or power failure

Rest periods, wash-up time

● Physical working conditions

Age of plant and equipment

Housekeeping and sanitation

Light, ventilation, dust, heat, noise

Departmental distribution of employees; condition of work areas

Lunch rooms, rest rooms, drinking fountains, cafeteria services, vending machines

Safety and health programs and safety committees

Provisions for first aid, doctors, nurses

Work clothing, safety glasses, shoes, and tools

Lockers and parking facilities

Experience with Occupational Safety and Health Administration (OSHA), state and local agencies

Security systems

- Benefits
    - Paid holidays
    - Vacations
    - Military leave
    - Jury duty pay
    - Clothing allowance
    - Bereavement pay
    - Educational opportunities and scholarships
    - Child care
- Leaves of absence
    - Maternity and parental
    - Sickness and disability
    - Personal
    - Educational
    - Family and Medical Leave Act compliance
- Insurance
    - Life, accidental death and dismemberment
    - Sick leave and disability protection
    - Hospital, surgical, and major medical
    - Dental and other plans
    - Workers' compensation
    - Unemployment compensation
    - Social Security
    - Contributory nature of plans
    - Compliance with the Employment Retirement Income Security Act (ERISA)
    - COBRA notification procedures
    - State continuation coverage notification procedures
- Financial incentives
    - Profit sharing
    - Pension (compliance with ERISA)

Credit unions

Loans

Annual, regular, or discretionary bonuses

Employee savings plans

Tuition contribution and scholarships

Parking privileges

● Training programs

For managers

For supervisors

For non-supervisors

Apprenticeships

● Employee publications and publicity

Employee handbook

House newsletter or periodical news sheets—extent of employee participation

Letters to employees

Annual reports

Local press releases

Suggestion system; awards

Audio visual programs

● Employee interviews and meetings; complaint procedure

Interviews of individual employees—scheduling; analysis

Plant-wide or office-wide meetings

Departmental or other group meetings

Formal complaint procedure—steps and final resolution

Alternative dispute resolution procedures

Informal complaint procedure—personnel involved, final resolution

Log of complaints and disposition; analysis of major complaints

- Employee activities

    Bowling and other sports

    Picnics, dances, breakfasts, dinners

    Plant tours

    Contests

    Community resource programs

    Volunteer projects

- Past and current investigations of employment practices by governmental agencies

- Unions and union activity

    History of prior union organizing efforts

    Current union activity—handbilling, calls at homes, letters, activity on employer's premises

    Election petitions pending

    Unfair labor practice charges pending

    NLRB proceedings, orders, court decrees or judgments arising out of prior and current labor union activities

    Extent of unionization in company

    Current collective bargaining agreements—unit configurations, other locations

    Employer's experience with strikes, boycotts, and picketing

    Extent of unionization in employer's industry—unions involved

The information obtained from this audit will identify weaknesses and help the employer determine whether its personnel practices should be modified or improved.

BARGAINING UNIT VULNERABILITY ANALYSIS

A preventive audit also should include a bargaining unit vulnerability analysis. NLRB statistics and union surveys demonstrate that unions are most successful when organizing small bargaining units. An employer should examine its structure to determine whether it is vulnerable to a potential union's effort to organize a part of its workforce.

The Board is empowered to decide the appropriate unit within which to hold an election for the purpose of collective bargaining. Although no strict rules have been developed in determining the appropriate unit, the guiding principal is whether the employees share a "community of interest." Thus, the Board analyzes such factors as similarity of wages and hours, common supervision, and interchange or functional integration of the employees. (A more detailed discussion of the factors considered by the Board is found in Chapter XV at page 147).

To analyze its vulnerability an employer should place itself in the shoes of a union organizer and conduct an analysis using the "community of interest" factors the Labor Board employs. The employer can then determine whether any segment of its workforce might be vulnerable to the union's "splintering" approach of organizing small units and adjust its business operations accordingly.

For example, an employer might increase the frequency of temporary and permanent transfers between and among departments and locations, consistent with business needs. Job functions can be combined and operations integrated to demonstrate cohesiveness. If a union then seeks to organize the employees by attempting to carve out a small unit, the employer can challenge the proposed unit as inconsistent with the Board's community of interest factors.

TRAINING SUPERVISORS ON EMPLOYMENT MATTERS

Supervisory training is a key element in developing a preventive employee relations program and in avoiding unionization. There is an undeniable link between a supervisor's general fair treatment of employees and their interest in seeking union or other outside intervention.

One of the most important concepts to develop in supervisory training is the necessity of treating all employees and applicants fairly. This includes training supervisors and managers to be objective when hiring and firing, in making job assignments, giving promotions, conducting appraisals, and administering discipline. All employment decisions should be based on job-related reasons and should be documented.

Every supervisor and manager should be familiar with the types of discrimination which are prohibited. Although state and local laws vary, equal employment opportunity ("EEO") training should emphasize that discrimination based on race, sex, age, national origin, religion, or disability is illegal. The training should also alert supervisors and managers that retaliation against employees for exercising rights under a host of civil rights (and other) laws—especially the right to complain to a government agency even if the complaint is meritless—is prohibited.

EEO training should include a thorough discussion of the types of conduct or statements which may constitute sexual harassment and the methods by which supervisors and management may avoid employer liability. Employers should distribute sexual harassment policies to each supervisor and manager and, as the law changes or as circumstances require, update them.

Other complex areas of the law are family and medical leave and the treatment of disabilities. Training should focus on the basic provisions of the Family and Medical Leave Act, the Americans With Disabilities Act, and other state and local laws which govern leave requests. Training should concentrate on helping the supervisor or manager evaluate when a leave request should be referred to upper management.

In addition, it is important that managers and supervisors are trained on issues such as substance abuse, drug testing and discipline, employee privacy, safety, contagious diseases, and work and family conflicts. Workplace violence has become a serious concern. Supervisors and managers should be trained to document all incidents and to take appropriate action when warranted. Training should include a discussion of the legal concepts of "negligent hiring" and "negligent retention," which impose liability on employers with knowledge of an employee's propensity for acting in a violent manner.

While supervisors and managers are not expected to become employment lawyers, they must have a general understanding of these issues and how to recognize them so they know when to notify upper management or a human resources professional. The cost of keeping supervisors aware of their legal responsibilities across a range of employment laws and regulations is negligible in comparison to the cost of failing to do so. Other important elements of a preventive employee relations program are discussed in the chapters that follow.

CHAPTER IV

INTRODUCTION TO ALTERNATIVE DISPUTE RESOLUTION PROCEDURES IN EMPLOYMENT

Many non-union employers have had an "open door" policy for handling employee complaints, allowing employees to bring problems to their supervisors or managers. In recent years, however, employees increasingly have opted to consult an attorney, file a discrimination charge, air their disputes in the press or television, or seek help from a union rather than avail themselves of the opportunity to resolve an employment problem internally. This tendency to bypass the "open door" underscores a serious gap between management's perception and reality. It has contributed to the explosion of employment litigation, costing American businesses millions of dollars.

A trend is rapidly developing in the United States and throughout the world: the implementation of alternative dispute resolution ("ADR") procedures. Its purpose is to resolve quickly and efficiently disputes outside the courtroom, thereby reducing the costs of litigation. In the employment context, ADR encourages (or, in some cases, requires) employees to resolve problems through a variety of private dispute resolution mechanisms. ADR also is an important ingredient of a preventive employee relations program and enables the employer effectively to refute union claims that a collective bargaining contract's grievance and arbitration procedure is the only method for resolving employee complaints.

The simplest and most common form of ADR is the multi-step complaint resolution procedure described in **Illustration No. 1** at page 20. Other mechanisms include mediation, arbitration, ombudsman, and peer review panels. These methods may be used individually or in combination.

Illustration No. 2 at page 21, describes a typical complaint resolution procedure which includes arbitration as a final step. It should be noted that these procedures permit resolution of potentially all employment related disputes. Some employers may wish to limit their applicability only to terminations and other claims, such as sexual harassment, where exposure to jury awards is the greatest.

To be binding, the private resolution procedure must be communicated to all employees either as a separate policy or through inclusion in an employee handbook. Management should be sure employees know how to use the procedure and feel confident they will receive fair and impartial treatment. Additionally, all supervisors and managers should be trained on how the process works and the role they play in it. Where the handbook receipt states that the handbook does not create an employment contract (see Chapter V, page 28), the receipt should cross-reference the agreement to arbitrate. For example, the receipt may state, "I hereby agree to arbitrate employment disputes as set forth in the handbook."

MEDIATION

Mediation allows the parties to discuss their disputes with an impartial person who assists them in reaching a settlement. The process is private, voluntary, and extremely flexible. The mediator may suggest ways of resolving the dispute but may not impose a settlement on the parties. The mediator often will help the parties evaluate the merits of their dispute, pointing out the weaknesses in each side's case and analyzing the risks inherent in litigation. In mediation, unlike arbitration, the mediator cannot bind the parties to any resolution. Since the outcome is "non-binding," either side may "opt out" if it does not like the process. A wide range of workplace disputes, especially those that do not involve monetary damages, have been resolved through mediation. Surveys show mediation results in settlements nearly nine times out of ten and roughly 80% of mediated cases settle on the first day.

ARBITRATION

Arbitration is the consensual use of a neutral third party selected by the disputants to hear the dispute and make a final and binding decision. It provides a private, cost-effective, and relatively prompt way of resolving conflicts. Employers usually are represented by counsel. To level the playing field, employees should be advised they also have the right to use counsel. The lawyers present evidence, examine witnesses, and make arguments. The arbitrator then makes a binding ruling that decides the case.

Prospective and current employees are encouraged or required to execute an agreement accepting final and binding arbitration (see **Illustration No. 3** at page 25). Since state laws vary, employers are advised to consult with counsel before implementing binding arbitration.

There are numerous providers of mediation and arbitration services. A comprehensive listing is found in the Martindale-Hubbell Dispute Resolution Directory (1996). The largest and best known provider is the American Arbitration Association ("AAA" or "Association"). The AAA's National Rules for the Resolution of Employment Disputes encompass a complete mediation and arbitration program, including the listing and procedure for selection of mediators and arbitrators. Because of its experience and reputation, selection of the AAA will bolster the perception among employees that the employer has adopted a fair and credible procedure.

If an employer intends to utilize the dispute resolution services of the AAA in an employment ADR plan, it must, at least thirty days prior to the planned effective date of the program: (1) notify the Association of its intention to do so; and, (2) provide the Association with a copy of the employment dispute resolution plan. The AAA will advise either that the plan is acceptable or suggest specific changes. If an employer does not comply with this requirement, the Association reserves the right to decline its administrative services. Copies of these plans should be sent to the American Arbitration Association's Office of Program Development, 140 West 51st Street, New York, NY 10020; Fax: 212-541-4841; http://www.adr.org.

OMBUDSMAN

The word "ombudsman" is Swedish and means a commissioned representative of the king. As used in the ADR context in America, an ombudsperson is an employee who assists other employees in investigating complaints and reporting to senior management on their resolution. The person is authorized to cut through red tape and obtain an audience with senior management, but he or she does not have authority to resolve any issues.

PEER REVIEW

Peer review is an ADR mechanism which may be used independently or as a final step in a multi-step complaint resolution procedure. Trained volunteers from both the rank-and-file and management serve as panelists. They are taught to be adjudicators and determine, through a hearing process, whether the company's existing policy was applied appropriately. Training should include how to listen dispassionately and objectively, ask relevant questions and evaluate the answers.

Typically, a panel consists of five people, three rank-and-file employees (*i.e.*, peers of the complainant), and two managers. Anyone who is related to the complainant or who might be affected by the decision or has some conflict of interest may be disqualified. Also, any manager who is in the direct line of supervision of the complainant should be disqualified.

The hearing is often facilitated by a human resources representative to assist the employee with his or her presentation and with all relevant documents. The employee presents the case and describes the relief sought (such as back pay, reinstatement, or a letter of apology). Then, the supervisor who made the original decision presents his or her side of the issue. If appropriate, the panel may call other witnesses and ask to see relevant company books, records, or documents. To keep the proceeding informal, neither party is represented by an attorney.

After each side has presented its case, the panel privately discusses the matter and, based on majority vote, issues its decision to affirm or modify management's determination, grant the complainant's request, or deny it. While the panel cannot change or rewrite policy, in some programs it may suggest to management that the policy be reviewed or revised.

Employers who have used a peer review system have found it particularly beneficial. Employees who understand and use the process are more likely to perceive they are treated fairly. Perhaps most importantly, an attorney will be far less likely to take on a discrimination or wrongful discharge case knowing that a fair and impartial system has reviewed and upheld the employer's decision.

Offering an ADR procedure such as peer review does not assure employees always will use it rather than resort to litigation. For example, a former human resources department employee of a San Francisco hotel brought a wrongful termination suit, notwithstanding a peer review-type procedure outlined in the hotel's employee handbook. Because of deficiencies in the procedure, a California appellate court held the employee still had the right of access to a judicial forum to adjudicate her claims. *Cheng-Canindin v. Renaissance Hotel Assocs.* (Cal. Ct. App. 1996).

JUDICIAL REACTION TO ADR

Despite some judicial roadblocks such as the *Renaissance Hotel* case, experience with ADR has been positive, and many courts have recognized its validity and efficiency in resolving workplace disputes. The rationale for doing so was forcefully explicated by one court:

The *raison d'etre* for lawyers and the adversarial process traditionally was to provide laypersons with affordable, expeditious resolutions of disputes. Yet, somehow in the development of the law through the last half of this century, the process became an end in itself rather than simply the means by which parties resolve disputes . . . . As a result, access to the courts now is neither affordable nor expeditious. In many federal district courts and state courts, years pass before an aggrieved party can even have the proverbial day in court. In the meantime, the process grinds along, inflicting staggering legal expenses on the parties . . . . [W]e have simply priced the court system beyond the reach of most citizens, because the cost of litigation far exceeds the value of the decision itself . . . . In short, our current legal system for resolving disputes is losing the respect of the public and is rapidly approaching failure.

* * *

Arbitration and other alternative methods of dispute resolution provide for ordinary citizens and businesses what our court system no longer produces with any regularity—affordable, speedy justice. *Bright v. Norshipco.* (E.D. Va. 1997).

In another case, the Court of Appeals for the District of Columbia upheld a mandatory arbitration agreement where it (1) provided for the appointment of a neutral arbitrator through the American Arbitration Association and the conduct of the arbitration proceedings in accordance with its rules, (2) provided for all the types of relief that would otherwise be available in court, (3) provided for more than minimal discovery, (4) required a written award, and (5) did not require the employee either to pay unreasonable costs or *any* arbitrator's fees or expenses as a condition of access to the arbitration forum. *Cole v. Burns Int'l Sec. Servs.* (D.C. Cir. 1997).

The willingness of courts to recognize and require the use of ADR procedures will spur more employers to consider adopting them. However, they must be carefully designed and implemented. This chapter describes alternative formats.

ADR is an important part—but only a part—of a comprehensive preventive employee relations program presented in Part I of the book. Other elements are discussed in the following chapters.

ILLUSTRATION NO. 1
SAMPLE COMPLAINT RESOLUTION PROCEDURE

We strive to provide a harmonious work environment for our employees. However, differences of opinion occasionally arise between individuals in an organization over what constitutes fair and equitable treatment. A complaint resolution procedure has been established whereby disputes can be resolved amicably, satisfactorily, and quickly.

A dispute includes any differences of opinion or dissatisfaction which arises from the application, interpretation, or claimed violation of any provisions of company policies, rules, or procedures, as well as any occurrence at work which an employee thinks is unfair. A member of the human resources department will be available to help the employee understand and follow each step of the procedure. We encourage you to use this procedure.

The following is the complaint resolution procedure:

STEP 1.   If you believe you are being treated unfairly, you are encouraged to discuss your problem with your immediate supervisor as soon as possible. The supervisor, after listening and investigating the problem, will provide you with an answer in a timely fashion. (Should your problem be of a personal nature which you feel may be embarrassing to discuss with your supervisor, or if for any reason you do not wish to take your problem to your immediate supervisor, you should speak immediately to your department head).

STEP 2.   If your complaint has not been satisfactorily resolved by your supervisor, you should promptly bring it to the attention of your department head. Your department head will provide you with a timely response.

STEP 3.   If you are dissatisfied with the answer provided by your department head, your complaint will be forwarded to the corporate president. The president and/or his or her representative will discuss the problem with you and investigate. The president will give you a timely answer.

ILLUSTRATION NO. 2

SAMPLE COMPLAINT RESOLUTION PROCEDURE
INCLUDING ARBITRATION

We strive to provide a harmonious work environment for our employees. However, differences of opinion occasionally arise between individuals in an organization regarding what constitutes fair and equitable treatment. A complaint resolution procedure including arbitration has been established whereby complaints, differences of opinion, or dissatisfaction can be resolved amicably, satisfactorily, and quickly.

A dispute includes any differences of opinion or dissatisfaction which arises from the application, interpretation, or claimed violation of any provisions of company policies, rules, or procedures, as well as any occurrence at work which an employee thinks is unfair. A member of the human resources department will be available to help the employee understand and follow each step of the procedure. We encourage you to use this procedure.

STEP 1. If you are dissatisfied with a decision of management, after discussion with your immediate supervisor, contact your Department Manager. To ensure that everyone's memory is fresh, we ask that you try to do so within twenty-one (21) days of the action you are complaining about and request a meeting. Your manager will meet with you and make reasonable efforts to resolve the issue. If you are dissatisfied with your Department Manager's answer or you do not receive an answer within five (5) working days, you should proceed to Step 2.

STEP 2. Put your concern in writing and submit it to your Store Manager within seven (7) working days of the Step 1 decision. (You may seek assistance from your Human Resource Specialist). If you are dissatisfied with your Store Manager's response or do not receive an answer within seven (7) working days, you should proceed to Step 3.

STEP 3. Submit your written concern to your District Manager within seven (7) working days of the Step 2 decision. He will carefully review the issue and respond. If you are dissatisfied with your District Manager's response or do not receive an answer within fourteen (14) days, you may request arbitration. To do so, the Vice President-Human Resources must receive your written request for an arbitration hearing within three hundred (300) days of the District Manager's decision.

The time limits in each step of this procedure may be extended by mutual written agreement.

Arbitration

● Initiation of Arbitration Proceeding

You may initiate arbitration by submitting a written notice for arbitration to the Vice President—Human Resources, with a check for $25 payable to the American Arbitration Association within three hundred (300) days following the termination of the preceding step. If you fail to submit a timely claim for arbitration within this time period, the claim will be deemed settled and you will be barred from arbitrating the claim. If the claim involves statutory rights, you must file it within the time limit established by the applicable statute of limitations. As the time limitations vary according to the nature of the complaint, the claim should be filed as soon as possible.

● Notice Requirement

The Notice should set forth the dispute, including the alleged act or omission at issue, your name, address, and home telephone number, the names of all persons allegedly involved in the act or omission, and the relief you are requesting. Within ten (10) business days of receiving such notice, the company will file a joint request for arbitration with the appropriate office of the American Arbitration Association, together with the applicable administrative fee as provided in the AAA's fee schedule.

● Selection of Arbitrator

The arbitration will be conducted by a single arbitrator chosen pursuant to the procedures set forth in the National Rules for the Resolution of Employment Disputes of the American Arbitration Association, as modified or expanded herein. A copy of the Rules will be furnished on request. The hearing will be held at a location mutually agreed upon by the parties.

● Date and Duration of the Arbitration Hearing

The arbitration hearing shall commence no later than sixty (60) days following the date of the selection of the arbitrator. However, the selected arbitrator may order the hearing rescheduled for good cause or if mutually agreed to in writing by you and by the company. The hearing shall last no longer than two days with each party having one day to present their respective positions. The arbitrator may for good cause extend the hearing and adjust the timing of the presentations.

● Representation

Both the company and the employee have the right to be represented by counsel of their choice and at their own expense. [Optional: If you notify the company that you will not be represented by counsel at the hearing at least thirty (30) days prior to the date of the hearing, the company will not be represented by counsel at the hearing.]

● Arbitration Transcript

The company, at its option and expense, may arrange for and pay the cost of a court reporter to provide a stenographic record of the proceedings. You may obtain a copy of the record by paying for the cost of the copy. You may also arrange for a court reporter at your cost if the company has not done so.

● Discovery

Discovery is a pre-hearing procedure by which you or the company may obtain copies of all relevant documents as determined by the arbitrator.

● The Hearing

You and the company will have the right to present evidence through testimony, documents, and cross-examination. Witnesses shall testify under oath.

● Post-Hearing Briefs

Upon request at the close of hearing either party shall be allowed to file a post-hearing brief. The time for filing briefs and the length thereof will be set by the arbitrator at the hearing.

● Arbitrator's Authority

The arbitrator shall have the authority to grant legal and equitable relief to the same extent as a court of competent jurisdiction. In any award of back pay, the arbitrator shall deduct any lawful setoffs from an employee's interim earnings, unemployment compensation payments, and any amount attributable to the failure to mitigate damages. The arbitrator shall have no authority to establish wage rates, wage scales, or benefits, review performance evaluations, or establish performance standards, work rules, or change company policies and procedures.

● Arbitrator's Award

The arbitrator shall issue a written award within thirty (30) days after the close of the hearing or the date for submission of briefs which shall include a written opinion stating the arbitrator's reasons for the award. The arbitrator's award shall be final and binding and may be entered and enforced in any state or federal court of competent jurisdiction.

● Arbitration in the Absence of a Party

Unless the law provides to the contrary, the arbitration may proceed in the absence of any party or representative who, after due notice, fails to appear or fails to obtain a postponement.

● Judicial Review

You or the company may bring an action in any court of competent jurisdiction to compel arbitration under this Agreement and to enforce an arbitration award. Neither the AAA nor any arbitrator is a necessary party in judicial proceedings relating to the arbitration. If any portion or provision of this procedure is held to be void or unenforceable, the remainder of these procedures will be enforceable and any part may be severed from the remainder, as appropriate.

● Arbitration Fees and Costs

The arbitrator's fees and expenses and the cost of the hearing facilities shall be paid by the company. The AAA administrative filing and hearing fees shall be shared equally by you and the company, except that you shall not be required to pay more than one hundred dollars ($100.00) as your share.

● Expenses and Legal Fees

The expenses of witnesses for either side shall be paid by the party requiring the presence of such witnesses. Each side shall pay its own legal fees and expenses.

● Mediation

At any time during the procedure either party may request the dispute be mediated.

ILLUSTRATION NO. 3

AGREEMENT TO ABIDE BY MANDATORY ARBITRATION

I have received and read carefully the (Name of Company) Complaint Resolution and Arbitration Procedure ("the Arbitration Procedure"). In consideration for and as a material condition of my employment and its continuation, I agree:

- To abide by, and be bound by, the terms of the Arbitration Procedure;

- That arbitration pursuant to the Arbitration Procedure is the exclusive remedy for the final and binding resolution of claims by me against the Company, its officers, and employees relating in any manner to my employment, termination of employment, or any term or conditions of employment; and

- This Agreement and the Arbitration Procedure constitute the entire agreement between me and the Company regarding the resolution of disputes by arbitration, and can only be modified, in writing, signed by the President of the Company and me.

THIS AGREEMENT DOES NOT CREATE A CONTRACT OF EMPLOYMENT FOR ANY PERIOD OF TIME, AND MY EMPLOYMENT REMAINS AT WILL. BY SIGNING THIS AGREEMENT, I AM AGREEING THAT ALL UNRESOLVED DISPUTES ARISING OUT OF MY EMPLOYMENT, WHETHER STATUTORY OR NON-STATUTORY, INCLUDING CLAIMS OF AGE DISCRIMINATION UNDER THE AGE DISCRIMINATION IN EMPLOYMENT ACT, WILL BE RESOLVED PURSUANT TO THE ARBITRATION PROCEDURE, AND THAT I AM WAIVING MY RIGHT TO A JURY OR COURT TRIAL TO HEAR AND ADJUDICATE SUCH DISPUTES OR CLAIMS.

- I have been advised of my right to consult with an attorney regarding this Agreement and have decided to sign it knowingly, voluntarily, and free from duress or coercion.

- My agreement to accept arbitration can be revoked any time within seven (7) days of my signing this Agreement, but such revocation must be submitted in writing to the Vice President, Human Resources and will result in denial of consideration for employment or my termination.

		(Name of Company)
_____	_____	
Employee's Signature	Date	

		By:_____ _____
_____		
[Employee's typed or printed name]		Date

CHAPTER V

THE EMPLOYEE HANDBOOK

The employee handbook is an essential communication tool and a key element of a preventive employee relations program. The handbook provides an introduction to the company, a uniform source of employer policies and employee benefits, and a common core of information for all employees. Handbooks eliminate uncertainty about company policies and benefits and reduce the risk they will be administered inconsistently. For that reason, even small companies will benefit from having a current and comprehensive employee handbook.

PREPARING OR UPDATING THE HANDBOOK

When drafting an employee handbook, management should review all existing written policies and manuals as well as any unwritten practices. Inconsistencies and inadequacies should be examined and corrected as part of the process.

Clarity and consistency in language and format are critical in drafting the handbook:

- The handbook language should create a positive perception of the company.
- The contents should be arranged in an orderly and logical fashion with topical headings and subheadings to facilitate reference to particular policies.
- Sentences should be kept short and overall writing style made simple.
- Terminology that is ambiguous or complex should be avoided.
- Each policy should be clear and concise.
- A table of contents and/or an index should be included.

Illustration No. 4 at pages 30 and 31, is a checklist of suggested topics. While every handbook must be tailored to the needs of the company and to the specific requirements of state and local laws, typical provisions include the following:

- **Letter of Welcome from the Chief Executive Officer.** Since most employees are interested in learning about the company's origins and founders, the letter might include a short statement about the history of the company.

- **Company Position on Employee Relations and Unions.** The handbook might include a statement summarizing the employer's philosophy regarding employee relations and unions:

    > Our success is founded on the skill and efforts of our employees. Our policy is to deal with our employees honestly and to respect and recognize them as individuals. In our opinion, unionization would interfere with the individual treatment, respect, and recognition we value.

- **Problem-Solving Procedures.** The handbook should also describe the company's philosophy and procedure for the resolution of employee problems, such as an "open door" policy or an alternative dispute resolution procedure discussed in Chapter IV.

- **Receipt and Disclaimer.** Each employee should sign an appropriate receipt for the handbook including a disclaimer acknowledging that the handbook does not constitute a contract of employment. This should be a separate tearout page kept in the employee's personnel file. Where the handbook contains a union-free policy statement, it should be separate from the receipt. The receipt should not condition employment on adherence to the employer's policies, which by implication would include opposition to unionization. *La Quinta Motor Inns, Inc.* (1989). See **Illustration No. 5** at page 32.

AVOIDING LITIGATION

A carelessly written handbook can be a minefield of legal problems for the employer. In recent years, the content of employee handbooks increasingly has become the subject of litigation. Employees often claim that handbook statements create contractual obligations which the employer has failed to meet. Properly drafted employee manuals can reduce the likelihood of costly and time-consuming litigation.

The courts of some states have recognized that personnel policy handbooks may form the basis for an implied contract between employer and employee in the absence of a clear disclaimer stating that the handbook does not constitute a contract. As noted earlier, a disclaimer should be included stating explicitly that the handbook and the policies therein do not constitute a contract. Where the handbook provides for arbitration as an alternative dispute resolution procedure, the receipt should cross reference the agreement to arbitrate. For example, the receipt may state, "I hereby agree to arbitrate employment disputes as set forth in the handbook." The disclaimer should be conspicuous and highlighted with bold, capital, larger typeface, or italics. See the next to last sentence in **Illustration No. 5** at page 32.

HANDBOOK TERMINOLOGY

Terminology common to personnel policy handbooks can also result in wrongful discharge litigation. For example, many handbooks refer to "probationary employees" who are subject to termination for any reason during the initial period of employment. This may imply, however, that employees who have passed their probationary period have some kind of job guarantee. To avoid the implication that employment becomes permanent and is no longer "at will," employers may wish to designate the period immediately following an employee's commencement of work as an "introductory period" and refer to workers who have completed their introductory period as "regular" employees, not "permanent."

It is important that the term "employment at will" be defined. If not, depending on the state, there may be an issue of fact for a jury as to whether the employee knew or should have known what it means to be employed "at-will." A simple explanation is that the company is free to terminate employees at any time for any reason, just as employees are free to terminate their employment at any time for any reason.

Care should be taken in dealing with another aspect of job security. Employers should avoid promising that an employee will not be discharged except for "just cause;" they may end up litigating exactly what "just cause" means. An employer has the right to set its own standards for employees. A failure to meet such standards constitutes cause for dismissal.

Legal and human resources issues have become intertwined; nowhere is this more true than with employee handbooks. It is critical that the employee handbook be prepared with expertise from both disciplines. Since employment laws vary from state to state, it would be prudent to consult with employment counsel when developing the handbook. The handbook's dissemination should be accompanied by supervisory training so that its full value is realized.

ILLUSTRATION NO. 4
CHECKLIST OF SUGGESTED TOPICS
FOR AN EMPLOYEE HANDBOOK

A. HANDBOOK RECEIPT WITH DISCLAIMER

B. INTRODUCTORY STATEMENT

1. Letter from CEO, including welcome to new employees and expression of appreciation to present employees

2. Overview of handbook, including right to make changes and terminate at-will

3. About the Company

   a. Aim and purpose

   b. Origin

   c. Products and services

4. Equal Employment Opportunity statement

5. The Company's position on unions and employee relations philosophy

6. Sexual harassment policy

7. Problem-solving procedure

C. EMPLOYMENT POLICIES

1. Supervisor's responsibilities

   a. Represents management to employees

   b. Represents employees to management

2. Introductory period

3. Hours of work

   a. Attendance and punctuality

   b. Time cards

   c. Overtime

4. Promotions and transfers (job posting/bidding)

5. Wages, salary, and earnings

   a. Area and industry comparison

   b. Pay day

   c. Payroll deductions

   d. Wage, salary, and performance reviews

   e. Shift differentials/premiums

   f. Commission program

D. BENEFITS
   1. Holidays
   2. Vacation
   3. Sick days
   4. Workers' Compensation
   5. Social Security and Medicare
   6. Employee benefit plans
      a. Explain that the benefit plan documents set forth the actual benefits. Summaries are provided for informational purposes only.
      b. Medical and hospitalization benefits
      c. Dental benefits
      d. Life insurance
      e. Pension
      f. Savings and investment
      g. Profit sharing
      h. Disability (long term and short term/salary continuation)
   7. Leaves of absence
      a. Disability (including maternity)
      b. Military
      c. Jury duty
      d. Bereavement
      e. Personal
      f. Family and medical leave policy
E. RULES AND REGULATIONS
   1. Substance abuse policy
   2. Smoking policy
   3. Solicitation
   4. Distribution of printed materials
   5. Access to premises by off-duty employees
   6. Safety rules and practices
   7. Use of bulletin boards
   8. Code of conduct, describing prohibited misconduct
F. TERMINATION OF EMPLOYMENT

   Employment-at-will statement (if not included in receipt)

ILLUSTRATION NO. 5
HANDBOOK RECEIPT

I have received and read a copy of the Employee Handbook. I understand that the contents of this handbook are guidelines only and supersede any prior handbook. The company and the benefit plan administrators shall have the maximum discretion permitted by law to administer, interpret, modify, discontinue, or enhance any policy, program, rule, benefit, or plan.

I further understand that the information in the handbook is subject to change at any time and without notice as situations warrant. Changes in any of the policies contained herein can only be made by the President or his designee and will be communicated to me by my supervisor or through official notices on the bulletin boards. I accept responsibility for keeping informed relative to any changes.

Neither this handbook nor any other company guidelines, policies, or practices create an employment contract. My employment is entered into voluntarily and is subject to termination by myself or the company at will (i.e. I may resign or be terminated at any time), with or without cause or prior notice.

_____   _____
Signature   Date

_____
[Print Name]

PLEASE SIGN AND DATE THIS FORM AND RETURN IT TO THE HUMAN RESOURCES DEPARTMENT.

CHAPTER VI

HOW THE UNION-FREE EMPLOYER COMMUNICATES

When an employer overlooks legitimate employee needs because of business concerns, it risks creating a perception of indifference to employee well-being. This perception, if not addressed, may cause employees to turn to a union with their complaints. Often, the underlying reason for poor employee relations is the failure to communicate satisfactorily.

Management may boast, "our door is always open," but this is often not the reality. Few executives have the time for people to wander in and out and even fewer employees have the courage to walk through the "open door" to talk to the boss.

An "open door" truly exists when employees have the means to discuss their problems freely with their supervisors and the confidence that upper-level management will be responsive to their concerns. Additionally, to be effective, communicating must be a two-way process. It requires listening—the key to understanding—as well as speaking.

SCHEDULED EMPLOYEE CONFERENCES

An effective way to find out how employees feel about the company and their work is to arrange individual conferences. Ideally, employee conferences should be conducted by a member of the human resources department or other management representative who is knowledgeable about the employees, their jobs and compensation, and the company's policies and practices. Individual conferences may be conducted at any time, but certain occasions present natural opportunities. These include:

- Change in job duties
- Change in rate of pay
- Promotion or transfer
- Anniversary of employment
- Recognition of service
- Scheduling of vacation
- Return from vacation
- Change of insurance
- Explanation of benefits
- Performance review

Employees should be encouraged to discuss their jobs. The discussion should be positive and emphasize suggestions rather than complaints. Generally, employees want to talk and will suggest improvements in working conditions, equipment, procedures, or benefits, in addition to expressing their own concerns. Although it may not be feasible to address every employee's individual problem, it is important to be responsive to every legitimate question and concern.

Individual employee conferences also provide an opportunity to discuss the advantages of working for the company. Thus, employees may be reminded of benefits they may take for granted or with which they are unfamiliar.

INFORMAL CONVERSATIONS WITH SUPERVISORS

One of the most important roles of the first-line supervisor is to keep open the lines of communication with employees. When supervisors fail to communicate, whether intentionally or unintentionally, employees feel shut out and may lose confidence that they are an important member of the team.

There is no magic formula for communications. Simply asking, "How are things going?" will easily open a conversation and often reveal matters of concern to the employee. These conversations do not have to be structured or planned. They may be held in the work area, the break room, the cafeteria, or similar setting.

Before they can be expected to effectively communicate, supervisors should be instructed on issues of mutual interest to management and employees such as changes in policies, benefits, business plans, or products. Employees appreciate when their employer shares information with them even when the information does not directly affect all of them.

Taking the time to discuss job-related matters and to show a friendly interest in personal matters creates an atmosphere where employees feel they are valued. Through the basics of communication—asking, telling, listening, and understanding—a foundation for a sound relationship within the organization is easily established.

Informal communication between supervisors and employees will develop when the supervisor:

- **Is available.** A supervisor who is unapproachable, never around, or whose door is always closed does not promote open communication.

- **Encourages candor.** Employees must feel they can be honest about the way they perceive things.

- **Rewards initiative.** Employees should be credited for the helpful suggestions they make.

- **Compliments good work.** When employees do a job well, they should be complimented.

- **Is open to criticism.** Supervisors should listen to everything the employee has to say regardless of how critical (and perhaps untrue) the employee's statement may be.

- **Handles each situation seriously.** Supervisors should listen to each and every employee problem with respect.

- **Follows through.** Once the supervisor has gathered all the necessary information to respond to an employee's question, the supervisor should communicate the information to the employee in a prompt manner.

- **Keeps top management advised so common questions and problems can be handled consistently.**

These and other communication techniques can and should be taught through supervisory training.

SMALL GROUP MEETINGS

Small group meetings can be an effective means of communicating. If initiated during an organizing drive, the Labor Board will consider them unlawful unless their format was the same as before.

Cases in Point

- A company president had a practice of holding large group meetings two times a year and small group meetings five times a year. Except for the occasional individual conversation, he never solicited complaints at these meetings. After a union began organizing, the president held thirty group meetings at which he discussed the company's financial status and solicited questions. At two of the meetings, the employees responded with questions and complained about a retirement plan, holes in the floor, defective fans, a leaky roof, poor bathroom ventilation, and additional relief on the production line. The employer subsequently instituted a number of improvements in these working conditions.

After the union lost the election, it filed objections. The Board ruled the series of thirty meetings in which the president solicited complaints constituted a significant departure from his past practice and that the president's solicitation of complaints on an individual basis was not adequate justification for solicitation at the group meetings. The Board set aside the election. *Carbonneau Indus., Inc.* (1977).

● In another case, a nurses union began an organizing drive at a hospital. Some months later, the hospital introduced a new communications program, which included monthly employee meetings with management "for a free exchange of ideas and thoughts." The names of the employees were drawn by lot and different employees from different departments attended each meeting.

After losing the election, the union filed an unfair labor practice charge alleging the hospital engaged in unlawful solicitation of grievances through the employee meetings. In defense, the hospital argued the meetings were merely a continuation of its long standing practice of holding regular monthly departmental meetings.

The Labor Board disagreed, holding that, unlike the earlier departmental meetings which included only employees from the same department, the current meetings included employees from different departments and, unlike the earlier departmental meetings, the current meetings were designed to give employees an opportunity to discuss ideas with and ask questions of members of top hospital management. The Board held the monthly employee meetings were not a continuation of a prior practice and were unlawful. *Middletown Hosp. Ass'n* (1986).

An employer committed to a policy of communicating with employees through individual and group meetings on a continuing basis has the key to an effective preventive employee relations program. Employees who feel their problems and complaints have been heard and addressed by management are less likely to seek the assistance of a union or other outsiders.

Some employers have established more sophisticated systems for communicating with employees and seeking their involvement in issues affecting their employment. These employee participation programs are the subject of the next chapter.

CHAPTER VII

EMPLOYEE PARTICIPATION PROGRAMS AS A COMMUNICATIONS TOOL

Employee participation programs ("EPPs") can be an important part of a communication program. They provide a means for employers to inform employees about business-related activities such as organizational plans, new products, and sales forecasts as well as explain and discuss company policies and benefit programs. They also provide a vehicle for employees to voice their opinions regarding a wide range of employment issues including job restructuring, terms and conditions of employment, as well as to offer creative solutions for operational problems.

STRUCTURE

The way EPPs are structured is important to assure they pass legal muster and are effective communication mechanisms. Since employees are usually most comfortable in small groups, meeting with six to eight employees at a time is most effective. If the groups are much smaller, employees feel singled out, and if much larger, the meetings become unwieldy and discussion is inhibited. Employees may be selected to attend by department, alphabetically, or on some other random basis.

Meetings should be limited in duration. If discussions of matters are not completed, they can be held over to a later date. Formal minutes are not desirable, but notes should be made of matters that require follow-up. The employer need not have an immediate answer to every inquiry, but timely, responsive replies will insure the success of the program.

The selection of the person to lead the meetings merits careful consideration. Preferably, the discussion leader should not be a top-level manager. Yet, the leader must have sufficient stature to command the employees' respect. The discussion leader must be trustworthy, tactful, level-headed, and a good listener and must know the employees and be familiar with their work. A human resources manager or assistant often has these qualifications.

It is essential that the supervisory staff support this program. Supervisors and managers should receive training on the purpose and functions of the program, as well as the mechanics, and they should understand that the group meetings are not an attempt to undermine their authority. Supervisors should be advised of problems involving their areas of responsibility and they should have an opportunity for follow-up.

OVERCOMING UNION CHALLENGES

Studies have found that employee participation programs have been an effective deterrent to unionization. Knowing this, unions often challenge their legality, claiming they are unlawful employer-dominated or supported "labor organizations." See, for example, *Electromation, Inc.* (1992), enf'd (7th Cir. 1994). To minimize the risk of such a challenge, it is advisable to have employees rotate into and out of the groups. The rotation will provide a strong argument against any claim that the group is a labor organization. This type of employee participation program has been upheld by the Labor Board and the courts.

Cases in Point

● *Sears, Roebuck*

Sears maintained a number of retail stores in the Oklahoma City area. It also operated a central appliance repair service center that had ten departments. To address communication problems that had arisen among some of the employees, particularly between the parts department and outside technicians, and to help them better understand each other's jobs, the company established a "communication committee." The committee was comprised of one employee from each department who met with the center's operations manager at two successive committee meetings. By using this rotating system, all employees in each department had an opportunity to participate in at least two committee meetings.

Some months later, the International Union of Electrical, Radio and Machine Workers filed an unfair labor practice charge against Sears, claiming that the communications committee was an unlawful labor organization. Following a hearing, an administrative law judge dismissed the charge, stating:

The communications committee was not an employee representative or advocate. The committee did not deal with the Company on behalf of the employees. The employees on the committee were not selected by their fellow employees and they did not represent their fellow employees. All the employees, on a rotation basis, were to participate in meetings with management to give input in order to help solve management problems. I therefore find that the communications committee was not a labor organization within the meaning of the Act.

Upon review, the Labor Board upheld the judge's finding that the communications committee was not a labor organization. *Sears, Roebuck & Co.* (1985).

● *Scott & Fetzer*

Similarly, a U.S. appeals court held that a plant committee was not a labor organization where rotating employee members participated no more than three times in a calendar year. Viewing the committee as nothing more than a communication device, the court stated:

The continuous rotation of committee members to ensure that many employees participate makes the committee resemble more closely the employee groups speaking directly to management on an individual, rather than a representative, basis. . . . *NLRB v. Streamway Div. of the Scott & Fetzer Co.* (6th Cir. 1982).

● *Peninsula General Hospital*

Another federal appeals court denied enforcement of a Board order to disestablish a nurses' committee. The Board had held that the committee, the Nursing Services Organization, unlawfully dealt with the hospital concerning matters affecting the nurses' employment. The court noted that "the critical question" in most cases involving an allegation that an employee committee is an employer-dominated "labor organization" is whether the committee "deals with" the employer. In addressing this question, the court set forth the following general principles:

(1) An employer does not necessarily "deal with" its employees merely by communicating with them, even if the matters addressed concern working conditions;

(2) "Dealing" occurs only if there is a "pattern or practice" over time of employee proposals concerning working conditions coupled with management consideration of the proposals;

(3) Isolated instances of the conduct described in (2) do not constitute "dealing;" and

(4) Management, in certain circumstances, may gather information from employees about working conditions and may even act on that information without necessarily "dealing" with them.

Holding that the committee did not engage in a pattern or practice of making proposals to which the hospital responded, the court concluded that the committee did not "deal with" the hospital and existed only for the purpose of communication. *NLRB v. Peninsula Gen. Hosp. Med. Ctr.* (4th Cir. 1994).

PREVENTIVE TIPS FOR ESTABLISHING A LAWFUL EPP

● Timing is critical. Do not establish an employee communication program as a device to defeat an organizing drive. If the Labor Board finds that the program was established in the face of union activity, it may conclude that the employer's sole purpose was to thwart that activity. The Board would then hold the plan illegal even though it was otherwise lawful.

● Committee members should not act as representatives of other employees nor use the meetings to present the complaints of other employees. The members should speak for themselves.

● Do not negotiate with employees or make joint decisions regarding terms and conditions of employment.

● The committee should not make formal proposals, but members may make suggestions individually.

● *The members of the committee should rotate.*

By following these guidelines, management will have structured a lawful employee participation program, joining thousands of other employers whose employees benefit from their use.

PART II

THE EARLY STAGES

CHAPTER VIII

EMPLOYEE SELF HELP THROUGH PROTECTED CONCERTED ACTIVITY

As noted in the preceding chapters, an employer's failure to provide an effective means for employees to air grievances often leads to their seeking union representation. Even without the aid of a union, employees may seek to resolve workplace problems on their own through self help. When they do, they are acting within the protection of the National Labor Relations Act. Section 7 states in relevant part:

> Employees shall have the right to self-organization, to form, join, or assist labor organizations, to bargain collectively through representatives of their own choosing, and *to engage in other concerted activities for the purpose of* collective bargaining or other *mutual aid or protection,* and [employees] shall also have the right to refrain from any or all such activities . . . . (emphasis added).

An employer violates the Act by disciplining an employee for exercising his or her right to engage in protected concerted activities. Conversely, an employer is free to discipline an employee for engaging in activity which is *not* protected by section 7. Determining whether employee activity falls within or without section 7 has been the basis for hundreds of sometimes seemingly inconsistent Board and court decisions.

The term "protected concerted activities" usually refers to two or more employees acting together toward a lawful common goal countenanced by the Act. However, the phrase is not confined to this meaning and, under some circumstances, can include individual activity. The following cases are illustrative of group and individual activity.

GROUP ACTION AS PROTECTED CONCERTED ACTIVITY

Refusal to Work Due to Unsatisfactory Conditions

Several employees of the Washington Aluminum Company had been complaining individually to management about the lack of heat. On one especially cold morning, without notifying any member of management, seven employees walked off their jobs in unison and were promptly discharged. The Supreme Court held that, although the Act permits an employer to discharge employees for cause, an employer is not at liberty to punish a person for engaging in concerted activities protected by section 7 of the Act. The Court held that the employees' walkout was protected concerted activity and directed their reinstatement with back pay. *NLRB v. Washington Aluminum Co.* (U.S. 1962).

Similarly, seven employees of an engineering firm walked off their jobs to protest unsafe working conditions and were discharged. The Labor Board and the U.S. Court of Appeals for the Fifth Circuit held they were engaged in protected concerted activities and their discharges unlawful. *McEver Eng'g* (1985), *enf'd* (5th Cir. 1986).

Refusal to Work Overtime

Five employees of Polytech, a manufacturer of transparent plastic sheets, refused to work overtime, claiming they were tired. Each received a two day suspension. The Labor Board held that a single concerted refusal to work overtime is protected concerted activity; the company's disciplinary action was unlawful. *Polytech, Inc.* (1972).

Refusal to Work Due to Attendance at Union Meeting

Thirty-four employees took a day off to attend a union organization meeting and were discharged. The Board held they were engaged in protected concerted activity and ordered them reinstated. *Robertson Indus.* (1975), enf'd (9th Cir. 1976).

Refusal to Work Due to Manager's Sexual Harassment

Downslope Industries was engaged in the manufacture and sale of ski garments. The newly-hired plant manager made verbal and physical advances toward women employees, speaking to them about his sexual prowess, inviting them to his motel room, and leaning over their shoulders and breathing down their necks.

The women complained to their supervisor who brought the incidents to the attention of the general manager. He responded that the plant manager was "only human." The supervisor told her employees they would have to talk to the general manager themselves.

The following morning all the employees gathered around the supervisor's desk, refusing to start work until they spoke to the general manager about the sexual harassment. Upon his arrival, he responded to their complaint by telling them "you're big girls." He then asked all who refused to work to raise their hands. When eight raised their hands, he said they either work under those conditions or "hit the clock;" he fired all eight as well as the supervisor.

The Board, affirmed by the U.S. Court of Appeals for the Sixth Circuit, held that freedom from sexual harassment is a working condition employees may concertedly protest for their mutual aid or protection. All, including the supervisor, were ordered reinstated with back pay. *Downslope Indus., Inc.* (1979), *enf'd* (6th Cir. 1982).

Protest over Employer's Failure to Contribute to Profit-Sharing Plan

A manufacturer of hair curlers and bobby pins had a profit-sharing plan to which it made yearly contributions to its employees' accounts. One year the company decided its profits should be invested in new equipment rather than contributed to the plan. This decision was explained to the employees by the machine shop foreman who also spoke individually to some employees. As a result of their reaction, the foreman called a meeting and solicited comments. One employee asked why the company had not furnished the employees with a plan booklet. Another said he did not like the company using his money to invest in new machines. Other employees made derogatory remarks about the company.

After the meeting, the employees returned to their work stations. One employee pounded on his lathe and shouted, "[t]his company is no f—g good, no goddamn good." When the president heard what had transpired, she discharged the employee who made these remarks and another who later filed unfair labor practice charges with the Labor Board.

The company argued the employees' comments at the meeting and at their work stations were not group action but individual griping. The Board rejected that argument and held the employees had been discharged unlawfully for engaging in protected concerted activity. This decision was affirmed by the U.S. Court of Appeals for the Third Circuit.

The court held that "'[m]ere griping' about a condition of employment is not protected, but when the griping coalesces with expression inclined to produce group or representative action, the statute protects the activity." Thus, it concluded, "the protests about the profit-sharing plan which preceded and followed [the meeting], and the questions raised and suggestions made at the meeting, are sufficient in our view to fit in the mold of 'group action.'" *Hugh H. Wilson Corp.* (1968), *enf'd* (3d Cir. 1969), *cert. denied* (U.S. 1970).

Unlawful Handbook Restrictions

A national operator of child care facilities had a rule in its employee handbook prohibiting employees from discussing terms and conditions of employment with parents. The handbook further provided:

> If you have a work-related complaint, concern, or problem of any kind, it is essential that you bring it to the attention of the Center Director immediately or use the company problem solving procedure set forth in this handbook. Failure to abide by this policy statement may constitute grounds for disciplinary action up to and including termination.

The Board found both rules were unlawful. The "parent communication" rule improperly prevented employees from communicating with third parties. The rule requiring employees to bring work-related complaints to the company, rather than invoking the assistance of a union or discussing the issue amongst themselves, restrained the employees' right to engage in concerted activities for their mutual aid or protection. *Kinder-Care Learning Ctrs.* (1990).

Complaints About Working Conditions

● A counselor at a small crisis intervention shelter for women and youths, along with two other employees, asked their supervisor about certain benefits following the shelter's merger with another non-profit organization. When the supervisor did not have an answer, the counselor telephoned the Wage and Hour Division of the U.S. Department of Labor. Two months later she was laid off because of budget cuts. The Board ruled the counselor was engaged in protected concerted activities because her phone call was a "logical outgrowth" of the original request by all three employees concerning the benefits. *Every Woman's Place* (1986), *enf'd* (6th Cir. 1987).

● An assistant to a company's health and safety administrator wrote a memo to the safety committee supporting a no-smoking policy. The memo was intercepted by a custodian who showed it to an employee who smoked. The employee wrote obscenities and personal insults on the document and posted it on the lunch room bulletin board. Another employee, also a smoker, wrote additional derogatory comments on the memo, made copies, and posted them in other locations.

After a brief investigation, the company fired both employees for writing "derogatory, inflammatory and false statements" on the memo and distributing it. The Board held both employees were engaged in protected concerted activities by inducing their fellow smokers to oppose changes in the existing smoking policy. *Morton Int'l, Inc.* (1994).

● The warehouse manager of a vegetable packing company told the employees on the day shift he was going to reduce their weekly hours to thirty-six. The employees protested that this would not give them enough time to finish their work, but the manager replied they would have to work that schedule whether they liked it or not. A few weeks later, the dock foreman approached employees on the dock crew and instructed them to work an additional hour. All four refused to work and were terminated for insubordination.

The NLRB's General Counsel filed a complaint against the company alleging it violated the Act by discharging the employees. The company argued there was no evidence the employees were acting as a group when they individually refused to work the additional hour. The Board found the employees' refusal to work overtime was a "logical outgrowth" of their earlier protest over the reduction in their schedule. The Board's decision that their actions were concerted and protected was affirmed by the U.S. Court of Appeals for the Ninth Circuit. *Mike Yurosek & Son, Inc.* (1992), *on remand* (1993), *enf'd* (9th Cir. 1995).

INDIVIDUAL ACTION AS CONCERTED ACTIVITY

Filing a Grievance Under a Collective Bargaining Agreement

A municipal garbage hauler was party to a collective bargaining agreement under which the employer could not require an employee to drive an unsafe vehicle. An employee was discharged when he refused to drive a truck he believed was unsafe. He filed a grievance, which the union declined to process. He then filed charges with the Labor Board which held that an employee who asserts a right under a collective bargaining agreement engages in protected concerted activity, even though he may act alone. The Sixth Circuit Court of Appeals disagreed and denied enforcement.

The Supreme Court, in agreement with the Board, held that an employee's reasonable and honest assertion of a contractual right under a collective bargaining agreement constituted protected concerted activity. The Court noted that "concerted activity" is not defined in the Act; thus "the precise manner in which particular actions of an individual employee must be linked to the actions of fellow employees in order to permit it to be said that the individual is engaged in concerted activity" is not clear. The Court conceded that individual actions only remotely related to the activities of other employees, such as personal griping, are not protected. However, where an employee invokes rights under a collective bargaining agreement his actions constitute protected concerted activity, since they affect all the employees covered by the agreement. *NLRB v. City Disposal Sys., Inc.* (U.S. 1984).

WHEN INDIVIDUAL ACTION IS NOT CONCERTED ACTIVITY

● Prior to 1984, the Labor Board held an employee who filed a safety complaint with a government agency was engaging in concerted activity because safe working conditions were matters of concern to all employees. The Board required no actual demonstration of common complaints; it simply reasoned any complaint to a government agency, such as the Occupational Safety and Health Administration ("OSHA"), could benefit others and therefore constituted concerted activity. *Alleluia Cushion Co., Inc.* (1975).

● In 1984, the Board overruled *Alleluia Cushion* and changed its position on safety complaints. Kenneth Prill, a truck driver for Meyer Industries, an aluminum boat manufacturer, was having difficulty with the brakes on his tractor trailer. He unsuccessfully complained to his supervisor and subsequently had an accident that was due in part to the faulty brakes. He phoned the president who asked him to have the truck towed back to the plant in Michigan. Protesting that it was unsafe to move the truck, Prill contacted the Tennessee Public Service Commission, which after an official inspection, issued a citation against moving the truck. Two days later, Prill was discharged because, in the words of a company official, "we can't have you calling the cops like this all the time."

The Board found Meyer Industries had not violated the Act in discharging Prill. It held that Prill had not been engaged in concerted activities, but had acted individually. On appeal, the reviewing court sent the case back to the Board for further consideration in light of an intervening Supreme Court decision.

For a second time, the Board concluded Prill had not been engaged in concerted activity. The Board adopted a definition of the scope of "concerted activity" used by another court of appeals:

[A] conversation may constitute a concerted activity although it involves only a speaker and a listener . . . [when] . . . it was engaged in with the object of initiating or inducing or preparing for group action or that it had some relation to group action in the interest of the employees. *Mushroom Transp. Co. v. NLRB* (3d Cir. 1964).

The Board concluded that since there was no evidence Prill had joined with any other employee or enlisted other support, his actions were not concerted.

Prill again appealed. This time, the court found he had acted on his own, without inducing or preparing for group action. The court held that although his fellow employees might benefit from his actions, it did not alter the fact he acted alone when he complained to his employer and state officials and when he refused to tow the unsafe truck. *Meyers Indus.* (1984), *remanded sub nom., Prill v. NLRB* (D.C. Cir. 1985), *cert. denied* (U.S. 1985), *reaff'd* (1986), *aff'd sub nom., Prill v. NLRB* (D.C. Cir. 1987), *cert. denied* (U.S. 1988).

Prill produces the anomalous result that a unionized worker who individually complains about safety or other matters under a collective bargaining agreement is protected under the Supreme Court's *City Disposal* case, while a non-union employee who lodges the same complaint about common concerns is not protected.

● Upon receiving a complaint from OSHA listing 11 violations, the president of a detective agency remarked to an employee, "I'd like to get my hands on the SOB who did this, I'll drive him into the ground." The Board held the president's remarks did not interfere with employees' concerted activities because it was only directed at an unidentified individual employee. *Pagerly Detective Agency* (1984).

● A business school employed an admissions representative who received a letter from the school stating she had been placed on probation. She asked a fellow employee whether he had ever received a similar letter and his answer was "no." When the school's director learned of this conversation, he fired the representative. The Board ruled the question to the co-worker was personal, did not rise to the level of a discussion about terms and conditions of employment, and was not group action. The complaint was dismissed. *Adelphi Inst., Inc.* (1988).

WHEN ACTIVITY IS CONCERTED, BUT UNPROTECTED

The fact that an activity is "concerted" does not necessarily mean an employee engaging in the activity is protected under the law. There is a line beyond which employee activity loses the statutory protection, as the following cases illustrate.

● A registered nurse had been supervised by the same person for most of her employment. When the supervisor retired, she was replaced by someone whose management style was different. The nurse's relationship with the new supervisor was vastly different and she was no longer given preferential treatment. Additionally, she was warned about excessive absenteeism and antagonistic behavior toward her co-workers.

Suspecting that her job was in jeopardy, the nurse spoke to other nurses about the supervisor, asserting falsely that she had been fired for abandoning a patient in her prior job, and suggested they speak to the supervisor about her managerial style. The other nurses were not interested. When the supervisor learned about her activities, she confronted the nurse who admitted she was seeking to organize the staff nurses. The nurse was suspended and subsequently fired.

The Board held that when the nurse sought to enlist others to protest she was engaging in protected concerted activities. However, when she spread false rumors about the supervisor's employment history she lost the Act's protection. *HCA/Portsmouth Reg'l Hosp.* (1995).

● The president of a hospital sent a letter to all employees advising them a layoff was contemplated. After receiving the message, one of the hospital pharmacists responded by sending an unsigned electronic mail message referring to an administrator's vacation home and ownership of a Mercedes-Benz. The message automatically appeared on the terminal screens of over one hundred computers in the hospital. Believing the message was a personal attack on him, the hospital's president ordered an investigation. When confronted, the pharmacist admitted sending the message because of his concern about the impending layoffs. He was discharged. The Labor Board ruled that the use of his computer to send a system-wide message which interrupted the work of other hospital employees was not protected activity. *Washington Adventist Hosp., Inc.* (1988). However, generally, an employee who sends an e-mail message is engaged in protected concerted activity. *Time Keeping Sys., Inc.* (1997).

● An employer held employee meetings to present its views a few days before a union election. During the course of the meetings, numerous employees stood up and demanded the right to ask questions. When they refused to sit down, they were escorted from the meetings and terminated. The Labor Board, affirmed by the Fourth Circuit, upheld the discharges since the employees had engaged in a course of conduct designed to disrupt the speeches. *J.P. Stevens & Co., Inc.* (1975), enf'd (4th Cir. 1976).

● A job applicant, who listed as references an IBEW organizer and an IBEW business agent, was hired and began an assignment at a health care facility. He immediately started talking with other employees about improved benefits. He also explained the concept of "concerted activity" and told the employees that, if they wanted something, more than one of them had to approach management.

Shortly thereafter, four employees, including the new employee as their spokesperson, approached their foreman and asked whether the employer paid prevailing wages, had a pension plan, and, if not, whether it would start one. The foreman told the employees to return to work, but the spokesperson answered they were engaging in concerted activity and would not go back to work until they had an answer. When the foreman again directed them to return to work, they did. A few minutes later, the group again approached the foreman and asked about a medical plan. They were again told to go back to work, which they did.

About an hour later, the four employees approached the foreman a third time and asked about a dental and an annuity plan. When the foreman told them to return to work, the spokesperson responded they were engaged in concerted activity and wanted an answer from the owner. The foreman then told him to pick up his check because he was fired. The fired employee then went to his car from which he retrieved picket signs stating "ULP Strike against Land Mark" and, with another employee, began picketing. The fired employee filed an unfair labor practice charge with the Labor Board, claiming he was discharged for engaging in concerted activity.

Finding the group's action was "intermittent strike activity," the regional director dismissed the charge. On appeal, the Board's General Counsel upheld the discharge. Noting that the fired employee was a union "salt" (see Glossary in Appendix), the General Counsel determined that the concerted action was part of a plan of intermittent action inconsistent with normal work performance or a genuine strike. Citing Board precedent, the General Counsel held that such recurrent strike activity is unprotected where there are more than two separate strikes or threats of repeated strikes. *Land Mark Elec.* (1996).

● A manufacturer of acetate fiber products offered employees a pocket flashlight and a voucher for a free ice cream cone after securing a large contract. Several of the employees ridiculed the gesture. One of them posted a letter on the company bulletin board mocking the ice cream voucher:

> The employees of New River would like to express their great appreciation of the 52 flavors of left over ice cream from the closed Meadow Gold Plant. It has boosted moral [sic] tremendously. Several employees were heard to say they were going to work harder together, and do better so we could have some more old ice cream. We realize what a tremendous sacrifice this has been for the management and will be long remembered.

After an investigation, the company terminated the author and his typist. The Board held the discharges were unlawful since the company knew or should have known the posting involved concerted action. On appeal, the U.S. Court of Appeals for the Fourth Circuit, reversed the Board, characterizing the letter as "mocking and sarcastic." The court held that an offer of free ice cream was not a condition of employment that employees have a protected right to improve, and therefore the employees were not engaged in protected concerted activity. *New River Indus., Inc. v. NLRB* (4th Cir. 1991).

● The Aroostook County Regional Ophthalmology Center ("AC-ROC"), a small medical office, employed several physicians to perform eye surgery and otherwise treat patients. The Center's non-physician staff was comprised of nurses and technicians. The main facility was located in Presque Isle, Maine, with additional satellite facilities elsewhere in the northern part of the state.

On one occasion, the manager, Dr. Craig Young, found it necessary to change the reporting locations of three nurses and a technician in order to accommodate an emergency surgical procedure. When the employees heard of the schedule adjustment, they expressed dissatisfaction over the inconvenience caused by the change. Their grousing to each other was within earshot of patients and, in one instance, only three feet from a patient being prepared for surgery. Upon learning of this, Dr. Young called the nurses and technician into his office and fired them.

The Labor Board held that the employees' complaints to each other concerning their work schedule change was concerted activity because the discussions could "spawn collective action." Moreover, although the employees spoke in the presence of patients in a loud tone of voice, their conduct was not so egregious that it lost the protection of the Act. The Board ordered the employees reinstated with back pay.

Upon appeal, the U.S. Court of Appeals for the District of Columbia disagreed with the Board's finding that the discharges were unlawful. The court assumed, *arguendo,* that the employees were engaged in concerted activity when they lamented their schedule changes in the presence of patients. Although the activity may have been concerted, the court held it was not protected:

> In the setting of a small medical office, it is inherently bad conduct for medical staff personnel to complain about their jobs while they are tending patients. Indeed, it cannot be doubted that such misconduct is extremely serious, because it has the great potential to unsettle patients. It is hardly reassuring for a patient, concerned over his or her personal well-being, to be confronted by a medical attendant who seems distracted because of displeasure over the work environment. Such grousing in the presence of patients is plainly inconsistent with the reasonable demands of caretaking, and, therefore, it cannot constitute *protected* activity . . . . Therefore, ACROC's firing of the employees who engaged in such behavior did not violate the NLRA, and the Boards' finding is unjustified. *Aroostook County Reg'l Ophthalmology Ctr. v. NLRB* (D.C. Cir. 1996).

AVOIDING LIABILITY

It is evident no bright-line distinction may be drawn between concerted and other activity or between protected and unprotected activity. The Board and the reviewing courts sometimes disagree where to draw the line. Indeed, the Board itself has changed its mind as members come and go.

Employers should also understand that other labor or employment laws may provide remedies, especially in cases of discharge or alleged retaliation. For example, under section 11(c) of the Occupational Safety and Health Act, an employee who complains to management about an alleged safety or health problem may be protected against retaliatory action even though no concerted activity is involved. This protection also extends to supervisors, who are not covered by the National Labor Relations Act. The same employee might also be protected under a state "whistleblower" law which provides remedies to individuals who are retaliated against for reporting hazardous or illegal working conditions or practices. Thus, the employer often will need to look beyond the confines of the National Labor Relations Act to determine its legal rights and obligations when confronted with employee protests.

The cases referred to illustrate failures in communication between an employer and its employees. With an effective communication program, including responsiveness to legitimate employee concerns, employees may not feel the need to take matters into their own hands. Of course, as some of the cases illustrate, employees may break off communications and refuse to work unless their grievances are resolved, no matter how unreasonable the complaints or their solution. If, however, the employers in the cases discussed had alternative dispute resolution procedures in effect, as discussed in Chapter IV, every one of the overt employee actions might have been avoided.

CHAPTER IX

WHY AND HOW UNIONS ORGANIZE

When an employer is the object of union organizing, management may wonder, "Why us?" Often the answer lies in deficiencies in the employee/employer relationship. At other times a union may attempt to organize a particular employer, not because of employee discontent, but simply because the union wants to add to its membership rolls. Whatever the reason for targeting a specific employer, unions have become more sophisticated in their organizing techniques.

The union's organizing objective is to obtain employees' signatures on cards that authorize the union to represent the employees in collective bargaining. **Illustration No. 6** at page 70, is a typical card. Obtaining sufficient authorization cards will enable the organizer to file a petition with the National Labor Relations Board or seek voluntary recognition from the employer. While authorizations from only 30% of the employees are required to file a petition, most unions seek to obtain signatures from at least a majority of employees (see, for example, **Illustration No. 7** at page 71). Union studies show that a union needs support from 65% to 75% of the voting unit in order to have a good chance of winning an election.

GETTING A FOOT IN THE DOOR

An organizer's first step is to look for a leader among the employees and to form an in-house organizing committee. Then, with the committee's aid, the organizer will seek to obtain the names, addresses, and telephone numbers of fellow employees. Employees who have signed cards will be asked to solicit their co-workers' signatures. (See the union letter to in-plant supporters, **Illustration No. 8** at page 72.) AFL-CIO surveys show that where there is an active organizing committee the union win rate is 62%, but in its absence the union win rate is only 10%. Unions employ various techniques to accomplish the goal of obtaining a substantial number of authorization cards.

Opinion Polling and Mail Surveys

One technique is opinion polling, which is widely used in political campaigns. By conducting telephone polls, the union can determine the employees' predisposition to unionization and identify the issues on which the union should focus its campaign. Typical questions are:

- What are the one or two most important things you would think about in deciding whether to support or oppose a union at your workplace?

- What are some of the advantages in belonging to a labor union; what are some of the things a labor union might do for you?

- If a union did try to get into the place where you work, would you support or oppose it?

Another method unions employ to identify potential members is to conduct mail surveys, asking whether employees are interested in forming a union (see, for example, **Illustration No. 9** at page 73). The survey inquires:

- Are you still employed?

- Would you be interested in someone calling on you in the privacy of your home to explain the union and its benefits to you?

- Do you think you need a union?

- Do you think your fellow employees need a union?

Questionnaires and Quizzes

Another effective technique is to mail employees a questionnaire such as the one reproduced in **Illustration No. 10** at page 74. It asks employees to state the wages and benefits they now receive. It then asks them what they think they ought to be paid, whether they think their union contract should have a strong job security clause, and what they think they should receive in hospitalization benefits. Through this technique the organizer encourages employees to believe that the union can obtain what they want, if only they will sign a union card.

The "employee quiz," reproduced in **Illustration No. 11** at page 77, is a particularly effective technique. It cleverly asks the following "loaded" questions and then exhorts the employee to "take the first step" and sign the attached authorization card:

- Do I have an effective means to dispute unjust disciplinary actions, discharge, or discrimination?

- Do I have true seniority rights?

- Do I have health and life insurance with dependent coverage and/or a pension program for which my employer pays 100% of the cost?

- Are my wages reflective of needed skills and the difficulty of my job?

- Do I help determine what good working conditions are and what mine should be?

- Have any of the wages and benefits that I am receiving for my job been guaranteed in writing, signed by my employer, and notarized?

Building on Current Membership

Some unions begin organizing by asking their current membership for leads. For example, a union in Boston conducted a survey, "Do You Know Someone Who Needs A Union?" The union asked its members to identify potential union members among relatives, friends, or neighbors. From these survey leads the Boston union claimed at least one successful organizing campaign.

A different approach was used by Local 400, United Food and Commercial Workers Union, based in Landover, Maryland. It involved its membership and awarded them points for their efforts, similar to the airlines' frequent flyer programs:

```
Signing Up New Members  . . . . . . . . . . . . . . 50 points
Getting a Signed Authorization Card  . . . . . . . 50 points per card
Completing a Home Call . . . . . . . . . . . . . . . . 50 points
Handbilling . . . . . . . . . . . . . . . . . . . . . . . . . . 35 points per day
```

The ten members earning the most points each year were eligible for an all-expenses-paid vacation for two at an exotic resort.

Use of Discrimination Laws

Unions frequently use discrimination laws as organizing tools. Since many work forces are now predominantly comprised of women, sexual harassment is an issue that is of particular interest to them. (See, for example, **Illustration No. 12** at page 78). Organizers bring the issue into the open through leaflets and educational programs and inform female workers that freedom from sexual harassment is a working condition for which employees have the right to organize. Increasingly, organizers are filing discrimination and sexual harassment charges on behalf of female employees, creating pressure on the employer because of the publicity, the possibility of an investigation by the EEOC, and the threat of litigation by the union.

Salting

"Salting" is a tactic used by some unions to make initial employee contacts. The term derives from the phrase "salting a mine," which involves surreptitiously introducing artificial ore into a mine to create the misleading impression that the mineral was occurring naturally. By analogy, a paid union organizer who is placed in a non-union job to organize the employees is "salted" into the work place. "Salts" are the labor-management equivalent of the Trojan Horse.

The salting procedure is relatively simple. A union-sponsored individual applies for a job. He or she will falsely state prior employment to hide union affiliation. Once employed and assimilated into the workforce, the salt's job is to engage employees in carefully directed conversations, weighing their responses, and building up a cadre of sympathetic employees. If a salt has successfully infiltrated and obtained names, the organizer will arrange to meet the employees, either at their homes or in a bar or restaurant. The organizer keeps a low profile and, more often than not, the employer is unaware of these conversations. The effectiveness of this technique was noted by the Supreme Court in the case of *Central Hardware Co. v. NLRB* (U.S. 1972):

> As a part of the organization campaign, an "undercover agent for the Union" was infiltrated into the employ of Central [Hardware], receiving full-time salary from both the Union and the company. This agent solicited employees to join the Union and obtained a list of the employees of the two stores which was about 80% complete.

In *NLRB v. Town & Country Elec., Inc.* (U.S. 1995), the Court held that paid union organizers applying for a job were employees within the meaning of the Act and, therefore, it was unlawful to refuse to hire or discharge the applicants because of their union affiliation.

Encouraged by the Supreme Court's holding that "salts" were "employees" and, therefore, entitled to the Act's protections, unions have increasingly recruited members to act as salts. In applying for employment, they openly list their union affiliation on the employment application. For example, at one company, 42 members of the Boilmakers Union wrote "volunteer union organizer" on their applications for employment and were rejected. The Sixth Circuit interpreted *Town & Country's* definition of "employees" to include unpaid union organizers as well as paid. *NLRB v. Fluor Daniel, Inc.* (6th Cir. 1996).

The law does not require that an employer must employ an openly declared union organizer under all circumstances. Where the employer had previously adopted a nondiscriminatory rule prohibiting employees from working two full-time jobs, it may deny employment to a full-time paid union representative based on its policy. *Architectural Glass & Metal Co., Inc. v. NLRB* (6th Cir. 1997).

In *Architectural Glass* a full-time paid field representative for a local of the Glaziers union applied for employment with the company. He left blank the space on the application asking to identify his current employer, but in a later phone conversation with the company he acknowledged that he worked for the union. The employer then refused to hire him.

In defending against the union's unfair labor practice charge, the employer claimed he was not hired based on its rule prohibiting the employment of an individual who holds a full-time job elsewhere. The Board rejected this argument but, on the company's petition for review, the Sixth Circuit denied enforcement, holding that "under *Fluor Daniel* . . . an employer can assert a legitimate nondiscriminatory reason for refusing to hire a particular applicant."

Making Home Visits

Organizers generally agree that visiting employees at home is the technique most likely to bring favorable results. According to an AFL-CIO survey of organizers, unions won 78% of elections in which the organizer made home visits. (Where no house calls were made, the union won only 41% of the time.)

The Director of Organization of one union explained the reason for this success in his testimony at an NLRB unfair labor practice hearing:

Q. As an expert with several years' experience in organizing, what different methods of organizing can be used?

A. One is passing out literature or handbills, with authorization cards attached; another is making home calls, talking to people in their homes; another is talking to employees in parking lots; another is group meetings, maybe in a restaurant or coffee shop.

Q. Which method, in your opinion, is the most effective for the purpose of securing a majority of the employees?

A. The home calls.

Q. Could you tell us why these home calls are more effective than the other methods?

A. Because the person you are talking to is more at ease and more relaxed if you talk to him in his home rather than if he is on the company's premises.

To engage in these visits, however, an organizer needs to obtain the employees' names, home addresses, and, if possible, telephone numbers. As discussed, this is one of the primary goals of a salt. Some unions are willing to pay for this information. In one reported incident, three union organizers were arrested for allegedly offering a clerk in a company's personnel office $1,000 for a list of names, addresses, and telephone numbers of production employees.

Unions sometimes use very creative techniques to get this information. In one instance, a union conducted a contest among the employees wherein the employee who came closest to guessing the number of beans in a jar would win a prize. To enter the contest, each employee had to write down his name, address, and phone number. Almost all the employees entered the contest.

ADDITIONAL ORGANIZING TECHNIQUES

Initiation Fee Waivers

The most common inducement to obtain employee signatures on authorization cards is the waiver of any initiation fee. While a union lawfully may waive an initiation fee, it may not limit the waiver to those employees who sign authorization cards before the election. The offer must be unconditional and applicable to all unit employees who sign after, as well as before, the election. See *NLRB v. Savair Mfg. Co.* (U.S. 1973); *B.F. Goodrich Tire Co.* (1974).

Associate Membership

Another recently employed technique successfully used by some unions is the offer of "associate memberships." Unemployed or laid off employees, or employees who work for a non-union employer, are offered benefits such as group health insurance and merchandise discounts in exchange for paying reduced dues. This technique makes affiliation inherently valuable and allows the union to attract individuals who some day may be willing to organize their workplaces.

Lawsuits as Campaign Tools

One very effective technique that unions have used to gain the attention and support of employees is the offer to file a lawsuit for back wages, sexual harassment, or some other alleged employer misconduct.

● The Teamsters were involved in an organizational effort at Nestle's Bakersfield, California ice cream plant. At a union meeting the night before the election, Ron Carey, the union's international president, announced the filing of a lawsuit for back wages on the employees' behalf. The union's lawyer who was also present stated that, if the lawsuit were successful, each employee might collect as much as $35,000 in lost wages and damages. Flyers reproducing portions of the complaint were distributed. Carey appealed for the employees' vote at the Board election to be held the next day.

After the union won, Nestle filed objections, asserting that the announcement of the filing of the lawsuit on the eve of the election improperly interfered with the election. The Board certified the union as the employees' representative and subsequently issued an order that the employer bargain with the union. The U.S. Court of Appeals for the Sixth Circuit denied enforcement of the Board's order on the ground that the conferral of free legal services by the union was a sufficiently valuable benefit to improperly influence an employee's vote. An interesting postscript to this case is that five months after the election, the district court dismissed the complaint for back wages because the union failed to state a cause of action. *Nestle Dairy Sys.* (1993), *enf. denied* (6th Cir. 1995).

● The employees at one location of a large hotel chain were the subject of an organizing drive by the Hotel and Motel Trades Council. Upon learning of irregularities in the payment of overtime, the union wrote to the hotel's general manager that individual employees might be owed thousands of dollars in back pay and then distributed copies of this letter to the employees.

At an organizational meeting, the union's counsel stated a law firm had been hired to represent the employees in a Fair Labor Standards Act lawsuit to recover overtime and other wages illegally withheld by their employer. The union emphasized that the suit would not be filed unless a substantial number of employees joined the action. Over 30% signed consent forms. The union then filed the lawsuit eight days before a scheduled Board election.

After the union won, the hotel filed objections, arguing that the filing of the lawsuit eight days before the election unduly influenced the employees. In a lengthy opinion, the Board noted the Sixth Circuit's holding in *Nestle*, but disagreed with its analysis. The Board stated that the provision of legal services was no different from other union benefits which the Board had never found objectionable, such as providing the services of organizers, economists, safety experts, and attorneys. All these services, held the Board, "bear directly on the question facing every employee in the voting booth . . . the kind and quality of services the Union might be expected to provide if it is elected bargaining representative." The Board concluded that the union's assistance to the employees in prosecution of the claim for back wages was concerted activity on the part of the employees and, therefore, protected by the Act. The Board overruled the company's objections. *Novotel New York* (1996), *appeal docketed* (1st Cir. 1996).

Corporate Campaigns

The corporate campaign is a difficult union organizing tactic to counter. One of the objectives of "corporate campaigning" is to pressure the company to accept the union or to take a neutral position with respect to its organizing. Corporate campaigns usually enlist the assistance of groups and individuals outside the workplace, such as other unions, consumers, special interest groups, government agencies, investors, bankers, community, civic and religious groups, shareholders, customers, creditors, and the press, to put pressure on the company.

During a corporate campaign, a union may also pressure the company by instigating government inspections, penalties, and lawsuits through federal and state regulators, such as the Occupational Safety and Health Administration, environmental protection agencies, equal employment opportunity agencies, the Securities and Exchange Commission, the Department of the Treasury, the Department of Justice—Antitrust Division, state building departments, state health departments, and local zoning and planning commissions.

Another area of potential vulnerability is the corporate power structure, where unions hope to embarrass, coerce, or cajole high-level corporate officials into explaining company actions, apologizing for omissions or errors, or declaring support for the union. Executives, officers, and "inside" directors are vulnerable to such pressure since the public, the press, and government regulators may hold them responsible for the company's behavior. Outside directors, as executives or directors of other corporations, also are susceptible to these tactics.

Unions also may pressure financial institutions doing business with target companies. Unions often have large economic reserves, strike funds, building funds, and pension funds managed by these financial institutions. By threatening to withdraw these funds, a union can try to force the financial institution to influence the employer to act on its behalf. There are many other tactics unions use during corporate campaigns such as confrontation at shareholder meetings, picketing the homes of corporate officials, and lawsuits to publicize their cause.

Perhaps more than with traditional organizing, employers must use imagination, creativity, and outside resources to develop and implement effective counter strategies. To assist them, many employers retain public relations firms to build and reinforce a positive image of the company. Under some circumstances, employers may sue the union, its officers, and other groups drawn into the fray, especially if they seek to disparage its products or services.

The Right to Organize Campaign

The AFL-CIO announced early in 1997 that it planned to spend part of its $30 million organizing fund on a new program termed "The Right to Organize." It cited as a successful model of the program a plant in Everett, Massachusetts, where it became the bargaining representative for 175 employees through a card check instead of an

NLRB election. While seeking recognition through card checks is not unique (see Chapter XIII), here the union obtained the company's agreement to the card check through a sit-down strike by thirteen community leaders, including a priest, a minister, and a Harvard professor. This campaign has been cited by the AFL-CIO as a model for other unions to use in attempting to organize recalcitrant employers. AFL-CIO President John J. Sweeney, who appeared personally, stated:

> Everett was a beginning. From now on when workers organize to improve their workplaces and employers try to crush them, we're going to be there just as we were in Everett.

THE ORGANIZATIONAL MEETING

As the campaign progresses, the organizer will announce an open organizational meeting at a union or fraternal hall, motel, or similar facility to seek additional signed authorization cards. Selling the union to a group of employees in this manner often produces tangible results. A typical meeting was described by a union organizer at a Labor Board hearing:

Q. Can you tell us to the best of your recollection all that you told the employees at that time?

A. I'll try. I introduced myself and my associate and described what we do and what our jobs were with the International Union, and why we were here—why we were in town, that we were in town because some people from the plant had contacted us through another source stating that they wanted organization.

I then described the nature of our organization, because I didn't think they were familiar with us that much, and I described our organization, what we do, what we stand for, and so forth. I then proceeded to point out the benefits derived by joining a labor organization such as ours. I pointed out the difference in wages, working conditions, fringe benefits, such as pensions, health, and welfare amongst other things, that we have these and have enjoyed these things for years in other areas where workers were organized through union organizations for the purpose of dealing collectively with the employer rather than on an individual basis.

I pointed out the advantage of collective bargaining as against individuals going into or appealing to the company for a wage increase or for other things they may think they might need.

I then described that in order to represent the employees, we would have to have authorization cards.

And authorization cards were passed out amongst the group and we read the authorization card out loud and told why we needed them, that in order to represent a group of employees, we must be authorized first by the employees through a signed card; that after we secure these cards, we would contact the company for recognition.

I told them that I would do that immediately after the meeting. We then collected the cards and we received thirty-one cards out of the thirty-two people that were at the meeting.

After the meeting was completed, we gave some additional cards to the several people that were there and they were to contact those that were not there and ask them to sign cards.

Q.   About how long did this meeting last?

A.   Oh, I would say about an hour and a half.

Q.   Can you tell us briefly what answers were made?

A.   Well, when they asked us about the Union dues, we told them there wouldn't be any dues collected or paid by anyone until such time that a contract was negotiated and ratified. We told them that there wouldn't be any initiation fees collected from anyone that was there working at the plant at this time, that the initiation fees and dues would be set by the members themselves, and not by myself or the International Union.

CREATING THE CLIMATE FOR SUCCESSFUL SOLICITATION

To supplement the authorization cards obtained through home visits, handbilling, and union meetings, the organizer will commonly form an inside committee of employee supporters, as previously discussed, who will solicit card signing among fellow employees. Initially, this is done *sub rosa* so as not to alert the employer. At a certain point in the campaign, the union may decide to "go public."

Preventive Tip: Promulgate a No-Solicitation Rule

As illustrated in the foregoing excerpt from a Labor Board hearing, an essential step in organizing is to request employees to solicit cards from their co-workers.

To limit employee solicitation of authorization cards on its premises, an employer should establish and publish a written no-solicitation rule. (Handing an authorization card to an employee is considered "solicitation," rather than "distribution of literature," for purposes of this rule.) Although a no-solicitation rule need not be in writing, it may be difficult to prove employee awareness of an oral rule.

There is a disruption of work when either the employee who does the soliciting or the one being solicited is working. Therefore, solicitation may be prohibited when either is on working time. A no-solicitation rule may state:

Solicitation by an employee of another employee is prohibited, while either the person doing the soliciting or the person being solicited is on working time.

(a) Working Time Defined

The term "working time" is the period when an employee is required to perform job duties. When an employee is not working, solicitation may not be restricted. Non-work time includes lunch hours, scheduled breaks, time before and after shifts, clean-up time, and time spent standing in line to punch out, even if the employee is being paid for these periods. (Rules that use the term "working *hours*" and "*company* time" to describe when solicitation may be restricted are presumptively invalid.)

(b) Promulgation

A no-solicitation rule, to be lawful, should be promulgated prior to a union organizing drive. Then, if a union effort begins, the employer may remind the employees of the rule. Even a properly worded rule may be found invalid if it is adopted to counter union organizing. This is so even if the rule is only posted, but not enforced.

(c) Uniform Enforcement

A no-solicitation rule must be uniformly enforced to be valid. An employer which prohibits union solicitation but allows solicitation for other purposes during working time may violate the Act. For example, strictly enforcing a rule prohibiting union solicitation while permitting widespread solicitations for a variety of charitable causes would constitute unlawful discrimination. However, infrequent, occasional, or isolated charitable or beneficent solicitations will not invalidate an otherwise lawful rule.

Note that it is lawful for an employer to enforce a valid no-solicitation rule while engaging in its own antiunion solicitations. *Reno Hilton Resorts Corp.* (1995).

Caution

The rule may not be used to prohibit union discussions unaccompanied by solicitation. To justify a no-discussion rule, the employer would be required to show that it uniformly restricts discussions of all subjects not work related.

Organizing Retail Employees

A retailer's premises are generally open to the public, unlike a manufacturing plant or hospital. Union organizers often seek to use this circumstance to their advantage.

(a) Store Solicitation

The organizers may enter the store individually, in pairs or sometimes in large groups using a "blitz" type approach. In a "blitz," they have been known to have as many as thirty people fan out through the store directly approaching employees. By the time the store's security or management personnel are able to control the situation, the damage has been done.

In general, a retailer has the right to prohibit store solicitation by an organizer. An organizer may be restricted to coming onto the employer's premises solely as a customer. Where the store contains a public restaurant, the organizer may be evicted if he or she does not use the restaurant in a manner consistent with its intended purpose. Thus, it is permissible for the organizer to meet with off-duty store employees in a public restaurant only as long as he or she does not move from table to table or speak to employees who are on duty.

Where the organizer enters the store for any purpose other than as a customer, a properly worded decal affixed to the store's exterior door will place him or her on notice as a trespasser, as shown in **Illustration No. 13** at page 79. The organizer should be asked to leave. Should he or she refuse to do so, the organizer may be arrested for violation of the state's criminal trespass statute.

However, a retailer may not wish to arrest the organizer for a number of reasons: (1) the lack of uniform enforcement of the store's no-solicitation rule; (2) concern that the arrest may have an adverse effect on employee morale (although employees generally interpret the employer's affirmative action as the correct response); (3) the possibility that the union may file unfair labor practice charges or initiate other legal proceedings; and (4) the absence or vagueness of a state criminal statute.

If the retailer is reluctant to take any action and the organizer refuses to leave voluntarily, the retailer should at least observe the organizer's conduct. Even where the organizer is lawfully on the employer's premises (i.e., as a customer on the sales floor or, in the public restaurant, using the premises in a manner consistent with its intended purpose), the retailer may keep the organizer under surveillance for the limited purpose of enforcing its rules with respect to store employees who are working. Observing and documenting the organizer's inside organizational activities is essential in preparing for potential legal proceedings.

(b) Parking Lot Solicitation

An organizer will frequently attempt to contact employees on the store's parking lot. The Director of Organization of a retail clerks local testified at an NLRB hearing how he does this:

> We try to sign employees up on authorization cards in the parking lot. We try to obtain their addresses and set up appointments with them to visit their homes. We try to familiarize ourselves with the employee's car. If we go in the parking lot and see an employee driving a particular car and his car is there, we can assume that he is not at home. Or if his car is not in the parking lot, then we would go to his home, or make an attempt to call him at home.

Today, most retail parking lots are not the property of the retailer, but rather the property of the shopping center or mall owner. In such cases, the rules of the mall—not the retailer —would govern.

The prudent retailer should review its property lines and establish a relationship with mall management and its security force to understand what the mall will and will not do to limit solicitation and distribution in mall parking lots and common areas.

Special Industry Rules

Solicitation may lawfully be prohibited in certain working areas of retail stores, restaurants, or healthcare facilities on non-working time. These are exceptions to the general rule that solicitation may not be prohibited on non-working time.

(1) *Retail Stores.* The Board has upheld a no-solicitation rule prohibiting retail store employees who have constant contact with the public from engaging in union activity in the store's customer areas during their non-working time, as well as during their working time. These customer areas include selling floors, as well as customer elevators, escalators, stairways, and corridors.

However, a retail store which enforces a broad no-solicitation rule in customer areas during both non-working and working time may be required to grant a union's request to reply to management talks against the union given on the store's premises. *May Dep't Stores Co.* (1962), *enf. denied* (6th Cir. 1963). To avoid this contingency, a retailer may prefer to apply the less restrictive general industry rule against solicitation.

(2) *Restaurants.* The Board equates restaurants with retail businesses where customers deal directly with the employees. Accordingly, it has held that a restaurant may prohibit solicitation during employees' non-working time in customer areas.

(3) *Health Care Facilities.* A health care facility may prohibit employee solicitation in immediate patient care areas, such as operating rooms or patient rooms, during working and non-working time.

The Board has refused, with court approval, to analogize a health care facility to a retail store. It has concluded that a rule which prohibits all solicitation and distribution in all public areas to which patients and visitors have access is too broad. Accordingly, employee solicitation may not be prohibited in the hospital lunchroom or cafeteria even though patients have access to these areas.

ON PREMISES LITERATURE DISTRIBUTION

The organizer also may recruit inside supporters to distribute union literature within the facility.

Preventive Tip: Promulgate a No-Distribution Rule

To restrict literature distribution in working areas, employers should adopt a no-distribution rule. It may state:

Distribution of advertising material, handbills, or other literature in working areas of this plant is prohibited at any time.

OFF PREMISES LITERATURE DISTRIBUTION AND SOLICITATION

A common organizing technique is to pass out union literature and authorization cards to employees as they come to work.

In *Lechmere Inc. v. NLRB* (U.S. 1992), the Supreme Court held that an employer had the right to post its property against non-employee distribution of union literature. Stating that the right of self-organization conferred by the Act extended only to employees and not to unions, the Court held there were only two limitations placed on the employer's right to post property: (1) where the location of the place of employment and the living quarters of the employees place them beyond the reach of reasonable union efforts to communicate with them (no alternative means of communication), or (2) where the employer discriminatorily applies its no-solicitation policy. Hence, an employer which permits solicitation by charitable and civic organizations may not prohibit union solicitation. The ban must be uniformly applied.

Preventive Tip

To ban a union organizer from soliciting off-premises, such as in the parking lot, the employer should post a sign similar to **Illustration No. 13** at page 79, stating that solicitation or distribution of literature on any company premises, including the parking lot, by non-employees is prohibited.

ORGANIZING BY OFF-DUTY EMPLOYEES

Unions sometimes encourage off-duty employees to enter the facility to solicit co-workers.

Preventive Tip: Promulgate a No-Access Rule

To curtail organizing activity on site by off-duty employees, an employer should establish a written no-access rule. A lawful rule is one that (1) prohibits access to the interior facility as well as the exterior working areas, (2) is disseminated to all employees, (3) applies uniformly to all off-duty employees seeking access to the facility for any purpose, (4) is unambiguous, and (5) is consistently enforced. *Tri-County Med. Ctr., Inc.* (1976). An example of a simply stated rule is:

Employees are not permitted access to the interior of the facility and other working areas during their off-duty hours.

Otherwise valid no-access rules have been rendered invalid when off-duty employees were permitted to enter the premises to pick up paychecks, visit on their days off, or wait for fellow employees to finish work. Likewise, a rule that denies off-duty employees access to outside non-work areas is invalid. Thus, an employer may not prohibit its off-duty employees' distribution of union literature on its parking lot. (The Supreme Court's *Lechmere* rule discussed above does not apply to employees, only to non-employees.)

* * *

Long before these organizing techniques generate significant open employee support or attract widespread news coverage, the employer should educate itself about the union—its leadership, constitution and bylaws, strike history, finances, and other pertinent information. We discuss this learning process next.

ILLUSTRATION NO. 6

We, the members of the United Food and Commercial Workers Union, Local 72, invite you to join us in unity and share in our strive towards **improved working conditions, wages, health insurance and benefits for all.**

Together we can accomplish this.

If you feel you need a union where you work, fill out and sign the authorization card below.

For more information, contact the Organizing Department at 1-800-635-6994.

United Food & Commercial Workers International Union
Affiliated with AFL-CIO-CLC
AUTHORIZATION FOR REPRESENTATION

I hereby authorize the United Food & Commercial Workers International Union, AFL-CIO-CLC, or its chartered Local Union(s) to represent me for the purpose of collective bargaining.

(Print Name)	(Date)
(Signature)	(Home Phone)

(Home Address)	(City)	(State)	(Zip)

(Employer's Name)	(Address)

(Hire Date)	(Type Work Performed)	(Department)

		Day	Night	Full-	Part-
(Hourly Rate)	(Day Off)	Shift _____	Shift _____	Time _____	Time _____

Would you participate in an organizing committee? Yes _____ No _____   · ⬭ 81

Please Seal and Return. No postage necessary.

ILLUSTRATION NO. 7

REGION 2 • UAW

5000 Rockside Road, #300 • Cleveland, Ohio 44131-2174
Phone (216) 447-6080 • Fax (216) 447-1719

NOVEMBER 1, 1994

Greetings:

We would like to thank you for returning your UAW Authorization Card. You have taken the first step in having a real voice in your future. We appreciated your support and confidence in the United Auto Workers.

The next step of the organizing process is to get a majority of employees to also sign an Authorization Card. This will enable us to petition the National Labor Relations Board for an election. Enclosed are two (2) additional cards. You can help by giving these cards to co-workers who may not have received a card.

With the help of the UAW, you and your fellow workers will achieve better working conditions and the dignity on the job that all workers deserve.

Again, thank you! If you have any questions, please feel free to call us at 1-800-ALL-4UAW (255-4829).

Fraternally,

ILLUSTRATION NO. 8

Union Letter to In-Plant Supporters

International Union of Electrical, Radio and Machine Workers AFL-CIO and CLC

Dear IUE Supporter:

One of the first steps in getting the National Labor Relations Board to order a union election is to have as many as possible of your co-workers sign union authorization cards.

As a supporter of IUE, you have been given such cards and asked to obtain the signatures of your co-workers on these cards. Under the law, a number of rules have been established concerning union authorization cards and the solicitation of signatures. I have summarized these rules for your information and if any of your co-workers have questions concerning the cards.

1. Every union authorization card which is submitted to the National Labor Relation Board must be *signed* and *dated*.

2. The National Labor Relations Board protects the secrecy of these cards and has consistently refused to let any employer see them.

3. The National Labor Relations Board makes a determination of whether there is at least 30% (called a "showing of interest") without any hearing so that the secrecy of the cards is further protected. The Board's right to make such "administrative" determination without a hearing has been upheld by the courts.

4. When you ask a co-worker to sign a card, this is called solicitation of union membership. You have a right during *nonworking* time to solicit co-workers on company property.

5. You have the right during *nonworking* time to distribute union literature in *nonworking areas.*

6. Nonworking time includes coffee breaks, lunch, and rest periods and similar paid nonworking breaks.

7. Nonworking areas include restrooms, cafeterias, changing rooms, and company parking lots.

8. The Company will be in violation of the law if it attempts to interfere with your lawful solicitation.

Fraternally yours,

ILLUSTRATION NO. 9

UNION MAIL SURVEY

TO ALL EMPLOYEES

GREETINGS FROM THE WESTERN CONFERENCE OF PRINT-
ING SPECIALTIES AND PAPER PRODUCTS UNION.

WE HAVE BEEN ASKED BY SOME OF THE EMPLOYEES TO
HELP YOU ORGANIZE YOUR PLANT INTO THE UNION.

AT THIS TIME THE UNION IS GOING TO TAKE A SURVEY OF
THE EMPLOYEES TO FIND OUT THE INTEREST IN FORMING
A UNION. IT'S BEEN BROUGHT TO OUR ATTENTION BY
SOME OF THE EMPLOYEES THAT THE PLANT IS IN NEED OF
A UNION NOW MORE THAN EVER. OUR UNION HAS A NEW
ORGANIZING PROGRAM TO HELP YOU. IT ALSO HAS MANY
NEW PROGRAMS FOR OUR UNION MEMBERS.

ENCLOSED IS A SELF ADDRESSED ENVELOPE. PLEASE AN-
SWER AND MAIL THE FORM BACK TO US.

THIS FORM IS CONFIDENTIAL

1. ARE YOU STILL EMPLOYED?

2. WOULD YOU BE INTERESTED IN SOMEONE CALL-
   ING ON YOU IN THE PRIVACY OF YOUR HOME TO
   EXPLAIN THE UNION AND ITS BENEFITS TO YOU?

                    YES___   NO___

3. DO YOU THINK YOU NEED A UNION?

4. DO YOU THINK YOUR FELLOW EMPLOYEES NEED A
   UNION?

NAME

ADDRESS

PHONE NO.

YOUR TYPE OF WORK

ILLUSTRATION NO. 10

QUESTIONNAIRE

WHAT DO YOU WANT IN YOUR UNION CONTRACT?

When the majority of employees vote for the union in an NLRB election, the union then becomes the exclusive representative of all employees in the voting unit regardless of whether they have joined the union or not.

To fulfill this responsibility it is necessary that we know what goals you expect to achieve. To negotiate a contract for you, we have to know where you stand today and where you want to go.

The following questionnaire is designed to give us some of these answers. Everyone is urged to complete the questionnaire and mail it in the enclosed envelope as soon as possible. The average time required to complete this form is 15 minutes.

INDIVIDUAL QUESTIONNAIRES WILL
BE KEPT CONFIDENTIAL

Section I

This section is designed to tell us where you stand today and to give us an idea of how much your insurance and pension will cost. We have to know where you are so that we may better understand how to get you where you want to go when we negotiate your union contract.

1. Date

2. Store Name and No.

3. __Male   __Female

4. Your birth date

5. Your marital status:

    — Married

    — Single

    — Divorced

6. Number of dependant children living with you

7. Ages of dependant children living with you

8. Is your job the only income in your household?

  __Yes __No

9. Do you consider your income essential to your household?

  __Yes __No

10. What is your present rate of pay?

 (If on commission explain)

11. What is your length of service with your company?

  __Years __Months

12. What is your department name and number?

13. How many employees work in your department?

14. What is your job classification?

15. How many hours are you normally scheduled to work each week?

16. Are you covered by your company's hospitalization plan?

  __Yes __No

17. Are you covered by your company's pension plan?

  __Yes __No

Section II

This section is designed to tell us what you expect to achieve through the negotiation of your union contract. A union's existence is based on the achievement of goals for its members. In this section we are asking you what those goals should be. If you wish to comment further about your contract, please jot down any thoughts you might have on this subject and return them with this questionnaire.

1. What hourly rate of pay or what rate of commission should you receive under your union contract?

2. Do you think that your contract should have a strong seniority clause?

  __Yes __No

3. Do you think that your contract should have a strong job security clause and require that your company submit proof to the union for any disciplinary action taken against you?

4. Do you think that any disciplinary action taken by the company against you should be subject to a ruling by an impartial umpire?

     __Yes   __No

5. How much life insurance should you have where you work?

6. Should your hospitalization pay the full cost when you or your dependents are hospitalized?

7. (a) How much sick pay should you receive when you are unable to work?

     (b) How long should your sick pay continue?

ILLUSTRATION NO. 11

UFCW LOCAL 881

UNITED FOOD and COMMERCIAL WORKERS INTERNATIONAL UNION AFL-CIO & CLC

9865 W. Roosevelt Road . Westchester. Illinois 60153. (312) 681-1000

AN EMPLOYEE QUIZ

A few questions for you to answer about your employer:

1. Do I have an effective means to dispute unjust disciplinary actions, discharge, or discrimination?
2. Do I have true seniority rights?
3. Do I have health and life insurance with dependent coverage and/or a pension program in which my employer pays 100% of the cost?
4. Are my wages reflective of needed skills, and the difficulty of my job?
5. Do I help determine what good working conditions are, and what mine should be?
6. Have any of the wages and benefits that I am receiving for my job been guaranteed in writing, signed by my employer and notarized?

IF THE ANSWER TO 3 OR MORE OF THESE QUESTIONS IS "NO," PLEASE READ ON...

United Food and Commercial Workers Local 881 has already won the benefits covered in this quiz, plus much, much more (dental and vision coverage, $2.00-deductible prescription drug coverage, numerous paid holidays, personal days off with pay, etc., all guaranteed in union contracts). With the collective bargaining process, there is no limit for the future gains of our membership. You and your fellow employees can also gain these benefits.

JUST WHAT ARE MY RIGHTS UNDER THE LAW TO JOIN A UNION?

The National Labor Relations Act (Taft-Hartley and Landrum-Griffin) provides the following:

Sec. 7   Employees shall have the right to self-organization, to form, join or assist labor organizations, to bargain collectively through representatives of their own choosing, and to engage in concerted activities, for the purposes of collective bargaining or other mutual aid or protection.

Take the first step. Fill out the attached Authorization Card and mail it today—without delay.

Upon receipt of your card, a Union Representative will contact you. Or, if you would like more information, please call (312) 681-1000 collect, and ask for Chuck Kalert, Bob Johnson, or Mary Pat O'Shea.

ILLUSTRATION NO. 12

SEXUAL HARASSMENT:

IT'S NOT FLATTERING.
IT'S NOT YOUR FAULT.
IT'S AGAINST THE LAW.

AND THE UFCW CAN HELP.

United Food and Commercial Workers
International Union, AFL-CIO/CLC
1775 K Street, NW
Washington, D.C. 20006
(202) 223-3111

William H. Wynn
International President

Jerry Menapace
International Secretary-Treasurer

Patricia Scarcelli
International Vice President
Director, Women's Affairs Department

Sexual harassment is a workplace problem that threatens the physical and psychological well-being of thousands of American workers, principally women, every day. It's also a family issue that touches the lives of many workers whose sisters, mothers, wives, daughters, and friends also are victims.

Studies indicate that three of every four working women have been sexually harassed. One survey reveals that one in every four victims is fired as part of harassment, and another four of every 10 victims quit because of the harassment.

Sexual harassment hurts job opportunities for women. Because harassment compels many women to quit their jobs, they lose seniority and often end up with jobs at the bottom of the pay scale. This contributes to the continuing wage gap between men and women.

The United Food and Commercial Workers Union is committed to stopping sexual harassment wherever it occurs, and increasing awareness of its nature and extent.

Sexual harassment isn't just a personal threat. It's economic blackmail and it's a violation of civil rights.

ILLUSTRATION NO. 13

Sample Nonemployee Solicitation Sign

SOLICITATION, DISTRIBUTION of LITERATURE, or TRESPASSING BY NON-EMPLOYEES ON THESE PREMISES IS PROHIBITED.

CHAPTER X

INVESTIGATING THE UNION

The more an employer can learn about the union seeking to organize its employees, the better prepared it will be to develop and stage an effective counter campaign. The first step should be an investigation of the union's structure and finances. The investigation should learn:

- Names and titles of local and international union officers;
- Number of members;
- Location of union offices;
- Bylaws and constitution;
- Dues, initiation fees, and history of fines and assessments;
- Salaries and expense accounts of officers and staff;
- Identity of employers with contracts with the union;
- Size of strike funds;
- Record of strikes—economic, sympathetic, or in contract violation;
- History of boycott activities, either self-initiated or in support of other unions;
- Record of unfair labor practices and violence;
- Involvement in media or corporate campaigns;
- Reputation;
- Criminal records of officers;
- Government investigations of the union or its pension and welfare funds;
- Record of injunctions, contempt citations; and

- History of charges or lawsuits against the union based upon sex, race, national origin discrimination, or other reasons.

This information will be useful in developing strategies and preparing material for the counter campaign illustrated in the chapters that follow. In particular, it is important to learn about the financial condition of the union, since unions are businesses and must get a return on their investment. If resources are limited, the union can probably ill-afford an extensive campaign.

What are some sources of this information? Foremost are other employers who have jousted with the same union or have contracts with it, who may be able to provide invaluable first-hand information. The financial reports the unions are required to file with the U.S. Department of Labor are readily accessible and will provide a rich source of information.

UNION FINANCIAL REPORTS

The Labor-Management Reporting and Disclosure Act of 1959 ("LMRDA") requires labor organizations to file reports with the U.S. Department of Labor. One report, known as the "Labor Organization Information Report" or "LM-1," must be filed by the union within ninety days after the date it first becomes subject to this Act.

The LM-1 report contains the names and titles of union officers, as well as the dues and fees it charges its members. The union is also obliged to identify particular provisions of its constitution and bylaws dealing with qualifications for membership, levying of assessments, holding of meetings, audit procedures, mode of selection of stewards and officers, and strike authorization procedures. Since this report is filed only once, an employer referring to the report should be careful to verify that this information is current.

Another report required to be filed by labor organizations is Form LM-2, known as the "Labor Organization Annual Report." The first two pages of this six-page report are reproduced as **Illustration No. 14** at pages 85 and 86. The LM-2 itemizes such matters as salaries of union officers and employees, expense allowances, and receipts from fines and assessments. Upon first filing the required reports, the union is assigned a reporting number. These reporting numbers have been compiled in the *Register of Reporting Labor Organizations*, published by the U.S. Department of Labor, Office of Labor-Management Standards Enforcement. Copies of the *Register* may be purchased from the Government Printing Office by telephone (202-512-1800), by fax (202-512-2250), or by writing to the Superintendent of Documents, P.O. Box 371954, Pittsburgh, PA 15250-7954.

Area offices of the U.S. Department of Labor's Office of Labor—Management Standards ordinarily have the reports on file. In the event an area office does not have the particular union's report or lacks some information, such as copies of the union's constitution and bylaws, the documents may be obtained by writing to the U.S. Department of Labor, Office of Labor—Management Standards, 200 Constitution Avenue, N.W., Room N5610, Washington, D.C. 20210.

UNION PENSION AND WELFARE REPORTS

The Employee Retirement Income Security Act of 1974 ("ERISA") requires administrators of pension and welfare plans to file annual reports and summary plan descriptions with the U.S. Department of Labor, Pension and Welfare Benefits Administration. These documents may be obtained from the Department of Labor, Public Disclosure Room, Pension and Welfare Benefits Administration, 200 Constitution Avenue, N.W., Room N4677, Washington, D.C. 20216. This requirement applies to all plans maintained by both unions and employers, as well as to jointly established plans. A study of these reports will enable the employer to compare its pension and welfare benefits with those offered by the union.

OTHER SOURCES

Newspapers such as *The New York Times* and *The Wall Street Journal*, magazines such as *Business Week, Newsweek, Industry Week,* and *Time,* as well as news clipping services are rich in information about unions. Additionally, computerized information banks accessed through the Internet or the various on-line services are helpful in tracking down, through newspapers, magazines, or journal articles, the activities of a particular union or local in newspapers, magazines, or journal articles.

The labor press is another important source. Most international unions have their own newspapers or magazines which are available to the public by subscription or through public libraries. In addition to print media, many labor unions maintain home pages on the World Wide Web available to anyone with Internet access. For example, the AFL-CIO has a home page at http://www.aflcio.org. Here one will find press releases, news items, reports, texts of speeches, details of various campaigns, and other information that may be helpful in gaining insight into union organizing tactics, issues, and strategies. Another source for union organizing strategy and tactics "from the horse's mouth" is the *Organizing Guide for Local Unions*, published by the George Meany Center for Labor Studies.

Industry trade publications often report on union activity and union election results. Additionally, employer associations, such as the U.S. Chamber of Commerce, 1615 H. St., N.W., Washington, D.C.

20062, and the National Association of Manufacturers, 1331 Pennsylvania Avenue, N.W., Suite 1500N, Washington, D.C. 20004, are good sources of background material as well as current issues.

Official government publications on union activities are readily available. For example, the NLRB publishes a variety of reports, including weekly summaries of decisions and monthly summaries of elections results classified by industry, with a listing of the companies and unions involved and the votes cast.

The NLRB also issues an annual report, summarizing its decisions for the preceding fiscal year and providing charts and statistics of its activities. The full texts of decisions by the NLRB and its administrative law judges are available upon request. A listing of all NLRB publications is available from the NLRB Division of Information, 1099 14th St., N.W., Washington, D.C. 20570-0001. Its web site address is http://www.nlrb.gov.

The U.S. Department of Labor's Bureau of Labor Statistics, Office of Publications, 2 Massachusetts Ave., N.E., Room 2860, Washington, D.C. 20212, has many informative publications available for purchase. State departments of labor may also provide relevant material.

Labor law reporting services available in most libraries are an invaluable source of business law information. For example, **CCH INCORPORATED** and its subsidiaries track, explain, and analyze business law, annually producing over 300 publications in print and electronic form for accounting, legal, human resources, securities, and health care professionals. **CCH** is located at 2700 Lake Cook Road, Riverwoods, Illinois 60015. The Bureau of National Affairs' weekly Labor Relations Reporter publishes NLRB and court decisions and reports on news and trends. BNA is located at 1231 25th Street, N.W., Washington, D.C. 20037-1186.

The information obtained from these sources will help the employer better meet the challenge of the union's organizing drive and gain the initiative.

ILLUSTRATION NO. 14

U.S. Department of Labor
Office of Labor-Management
Standards
Washington, DC 20210

FORM LM-2
LABOR ORGANIZATION ANNUAL REPORT

Form approved
Office of Management
and Budget
No. 1214-0001
Expires 12-31-96

MUST BE USED BY LABOR ORGANIZATIONS WITH $200,000 OR MORE IN TOTAL
ANNUAL RECEIPTS AND LABOR ORGANIZATIONS UNDER TRUSTEESHIP

This report is mandatory under P.L. 86-257, as amended. Failure to comply may result in criminal prosecution, fines, or civil penalties as provided by 29 U.S.C. 439 or 440.

READ THE INSTRUCTIONS CAREFULLY BEFORE PREPARING THIS REPORT. SUBMIT THIS REPORT IN DUPLICATE.

IMPORTANT

If a label is here, →
peel off the top copy and
place it in the same box on
the second copy of the form.

If label information is correct,
leave items 4 through 8 blank.

If label information is incorrect,
complete items 4 through 8.

1. FILE NUMBER

2. PERIOD COVERED	MO	DAY	YR
From			
Through			

3. If your organization ceased to exist
and this is its terminal report, see
Section XII of the instructions and
check here: ☐

4. AFFILIATION OR ORGANIZATION NAME

5. DESIGNATION *(Local, Lodge, etc.)*   6. DESIGNATION NUMBER

7. UNIT NAME *(if any)*

9. Are your organization's records kept at its mailing address?   Yes ☐ No ☐
(If "No," provide address in Item 75.)

8. MAILING ADDRESS
(In care of) NAME AND TITLE OF PERSON

NUMBER AND STREET

BUILDING AND ROOM NUMBER *(if any)*

CITY   STATE   ZIP CODE

DURING THE REPORTING PERIOD DID YOUR ORGANIZATION:

	Yes	No
10. Have a "subsidiary organization" as defined in Section X of the instructions?	☐	☐
11. Create or participate in the administration of a trust or other fund or organization, as defined in the instructions, which provides benefits for members or their beneficiaries?	☐	☐
12. Have a political action committee (PAC) fund?	☐	☐
13. Acquire or dispose of any goods or property in any manner other than by purchase or sale?	☐	☐
14. Have an audit or review of its books and records by an outside accountant or by a parent body auditor/representative?	☐	☐
15. Discover any loss or shortage of funds or other property? (Answer "Yes" even if there has been repayment or recovery.)	☐	☐
16. Have any officer who was paid $10,000 or more by your organization and also received $10,000 or more as an officer or employee of another labor organization or of an employee benefit plan?	☐	☐
17. Liquidate or reduce any liabilities without disbursement of cash?	☐	☐

(If the answer to any of the above questions is "Yes," provide details in Item 75 as explained in the instructions for each item.)

18. How many members did your organization have at the end of the reporting period?

19. What is the date of your organization's next regular election of officers?   Month   Year

20. What is the maximum amount recoverable under your organization's fidelity bond for a loss caused by any officer or employee of your organization? $

21. What are your organization's rates of dues and fees? *(Enter a minimum and maximum if more than one rate applies for any line.)*

	Rates of Dues and Fees	
(a) Regular Dues/Fees	$_____ per _____ *(month, year, etc.)*	
(b) Initiation Fees	$_____	
(c) Transfer Fees	$_____	
(d) Work Permits	$_____ per _____ *(month, year, etc.)*	

	Yes	No
22. During the reporting period, did your organization have any changes in its constitution and bylaws (other than rates of dues and fees) or in practices/procedures listed in the instructions?	☐	☐

(If the constitution and bylaws have changed, attach two new dated copies. If practices/procedures have changed, see the instructions.)

	Yes	No
23. Were any of your organization's assets pledged as security or encumbered in any other way at the end of the reporting period?	☐	☐
24. Did your organization have any contingent liabilities at the end of the reporting period?	☐	☐

(If the answer to Item 23 or 24 is "Yes," provide details in Item 75.)

Each of the undersigned, duly authorized officers of the above labor organization, declares, under the applicable penalties of law, that all of the information submitted in this report (including the information contained in any accompanying documents) has been examined by the signatory and is, to the best of the undersigned's knowledge and belief, true, correct, and complete. *(See Section VI on penalties in the instructions.)*

76. SIGNED: _____ PRESIDENT
(If other title, see instructions)
(_____) _____
Date   Telephone Number

77. SIGNED: _____ TREASURER
(If other title, see instructions)
(_____) _____
Date   Telephone Number

Form LM-2 (Revised 1994)   Page 1 of 6

ENTER AMOUNTS IN DOLLARS ONLY		FILE NUMBER

COMPLETE SCHEDULES 1 THROUGH 15 BEFORE COMPLETING STATEMENTS A AND B

STATEMENT A — ASSETS AND LIABILITIES

ASSETS Item	From SCH #	Start of Reporting Period (A)	End of Reporting Period (B)	LIABILITIES Item	From SCH #	Start of Reporting Period (C)	End of Reporting Period (D)
25. Cash				33. Accounts Payable			
26. Accounts Receivable				34. Loans Payable	8		
27. Loans Receivable	1			35. Mortgages Payable			
28. U.S. Treasury Securities				36. Other Liabilities	4		
29. Investments	2			37. TOTAL LIABILITIES			
30. Fixed Assets	5						
31. Other Assets	3			38. NET ASSETS (Item 32 less Item 37)			
32. TOTAL ASSETS							

STATEMENT B — RECEIPTS AND DISBURSEMENTS

CASH RECEIPTS Item	From SCH #	AMOUNT	CASH DISBURSEMENTS Item	From SCH #	AMOUNT
39. Dues			56. To Officers	9	
40. Per Capita Tax			57. To Employees	10	
41. Fees			58. Per Capita Tax		
42. Fines			59. Fees, Fines, Assessments, etc.		
43. Assessments			60. Office & Administrative Expense	13	
44. Work Permits			61. Educational & Publicity Expense		
45. Sale of Supplies			62. Professional Fees		
46. Interest			63. Benefits	11	
47. Dividends			64. Contributions, Gifts & Grants	12	
48. Rents			65. Supplies for Resale		
49. Sale of Investments & Fixed Assets	6		66. Direct Taxes		
50. Loans Obtained	8		67. Withholding Taxes		
51. Repayments of Loans Made	1		68. Purchase of Investments & Fixed Assets	7	
52. On Behalf of Affiliates for Transmittal to Them			69. Loans Made	1	
53. From Members for Disbursement on Their Behalf			70. Repayment of Loans Obtained	8	
54. Other Receipts	14		71. To Affiliates of Funds Collected on Their Behalf		
			72. On Behalf of Individual Members		
			73. Other Disbursements	15	
55. TOTAL RECEIPTS			74. TOTAL DISBURSEMENTS		

75. ADDITIONAL INFORMATION (If more space is needed, attach additional pages properly identified.)
Item Number

Form LM-2 (Revised 1994)

CHAPTER XI

THE EMPLOYER SEIZES THE INITIATIVE

The union drive is in an early stage. Union organizers are visiting employee homes, garnering their support, and collecting signed authorization cards. The employer has recently learned of the union's activities. What should it do?

Some employers fear that by expressing their views they will be acknowledging the union's presence and even may encourage employee interest. Pretending that nothing is happening, however, usually spells defeat. Indeed, ignoring the early signs of a union threat and failing to respond to it in a timely manner are major causes of lost elections. As many employers have learned to their chagrin, in the face of union organizing, silence is not golden.

The employer must seize the initiative and speak out while the union drive is still in its infancy. Winning an NLRB election undoubtedly is an achievement; a greater achievement is not having one at all!

Timely and effective employer communications may prevent the union from securing a sufficient number (30%) of authorization cards to file a petition for an election and may even force the union to abandon its organizing effort. Although the union's efforts may be resumed at any time, the employer will have an opportunity to remedy problems which may have prompted employee interest in the first place.

PRESENTING THE EMPLOYER'S VIEWS

Until now, employees solicited by the union have heard only one side of the story. Management has or should have a viewpoint on unionization and the employees should know what that is. Moreover, the employees should know that management is lawfully entitled to oppose unionization and that management is determined to mount a legitimate campaign to maintain its union free status.

Employees who are solicited to sign cards may not be aware of their company's position about unions. In fact, employees may have been told by union organizers that the employer is in favor of the union or that it is not opposed to it. It is imperative, therefore, that the employer express its position early, clearly, concisely, and persuasively.

COMMUNICATING THROUGH GROUP MEETINGS

Under most circumstances a group meeting with employees is more effective than a written communication. There are no prohibitions against an employer speaking to groups of employees at this time, even though this may not have been a regular management practice. A straightforward presentation of the employer's position on unions is best. It should be unequivocal and avoid subtlety. When discussing specific aspects of the union's campaign—the significance of authorization cards, for example—management should be factual and instructive.

Preparing a written text of the presentation, though possibly appearing too formal, avoids misinterpretations resulting from extemporaneous statements. The written text also may prove useful in refuting possible union assertions that the employer made unlawful threats of reprisal or promises of benefit. Moreover, if a union advocate surreptitiously tapes the speech and tries to use portions of it taken out of context against the employer, the prepared text preserves for management a complete record of what was said. Of course, the talk is usually more convincing if the speaker does not appear to be reading it, but the temptation to extemporize should be resisted.

The selection of the "right" person to give the talk is of utmost importance. Consideration should be given to the speaker's authority, credibility, and communication skills. Usually, the presenter will be the senior management representative of the unit in which the organizing is occurring. In a plant-wide unit, consider the plant manager; in a store-wide unit, the store manager. Sometimes, in a multi-plant corporation, or where the local manager is the reason for the union activity, it may be desirable to have a higher level management representative make the presentation to lend importance to the message.

AVOIDING PROBLEMS

One note of caution: in group meetings, employees often want to ask questions from the floor. Experience shows that it is best to state at the outset that questions will be answered individually following the talk. The speaker thereby may avoid the embarrassment of being forced to make an unprepared response to a "shop lawyer's" provocative and often union-inspired question. More importantly, deferring questions from the floor avoids a spontaneous response which may later prove to be of questionable legality. Where such questions are anticipated from known union advocates, the employees may be excluded from the meeting unless their exclusion results in a loss of benefits or overtime pay. *Wimpey Minerals USA, Inc.* (1995).

Infrequently, the employer may ask its legal counsel or consultant to make a presentation to the employees. See, for example, *Acme Bus Corp.* (1996). This should be avoided. The employer's managers and supervisors know the employees and should have credibility with them; an attorney ordinarily does not. Moreover, an attorney (or a consultant) who communicates to employees in an effort to influence the exercise of their rights to engage in unionization is required to file financial disclosure forms with the U.S. Department of Labor. See Labor-Management Reporting and Disclosure Act of 1959 § 203(b), 29 U.S.C. § 433(b) (1995); *Wirtz v. Fowler* (5th Cir. 1966).

Occasionally, a union representative will request the opportunity to reply to the employer's talk or to "debate the issues" (see, for example, **Illustration No. 15** at page 96). As a general rule, such requests should be rejected. A union organizer can make promises; the employer lawfully cannot make any promises, other than to give assurances that it will continue to treat employees fairly. Since the employer cannot "out-promise" the union, it may look like the "loser" in the debate. Nevertheless, in certain circumstances, the employer may want to accept the union's challenge, conditioning it on the union's waiver of any right to take issue with the employer's statements. (See the conditions set forth in the last paragraph of **Illustration No. 16** at page 97).

COMMUNICATING CONCERNING UNION AUTHORIZATION CARDS

Often, union organizers will tell employees that a majority of their fellow workers have already signed authorization cards, regardless of whether that statement is accurate. Usually the statement is inaccurate, particularly at an early stage of organizing. To counter such misrepresentations, employer communication is essential, such as in **Illustration No. 17** at page 98.

Another common misrepresentation by unions is the assertion that signed authorization cards will remain confidential. Typically, the union states in its literature:

> The cards are strictly confidential. The only people knowing whether you signed a card are yourself, the union, and the NLRB agent. In no event will the Company see, or find out, who signed or did not sign cards.

This is hardly the truth. Cards signed by employees are often shown to other employees to demonstrate the union's growing support. Also, the union sometimes shows the cards to the employer to support a demand for recognition. As one court stated:

> Union cards are not confidential material. They are executed *for presentation* to the employer. The remotest possibility of an employee's understanding that his signature is a secret should be dispelled . . . . (Emphasis in original.) *J.P. Stevens & Co., Inc. v. NLRB* (4th Cir. 1971).

Furthermore, authorization cards may be submitted into evidence at an unfair labor practice hearing as proof that the union represents a majority of the employees. This use of authorization cards to establish a union's representative status was sanctioned by the Supreme Court in the landmark case of *NLRB v. Gissel Packing Co., Inc.* (U.S. 1968). The Court held that where the union had obtained cards from a majority of employees, the Board could properly issue a bargaining order against an employer whose commission of serious unfair labor practices had a tendency to undermine the union's majority status and preclude the holding of a fair election.

Under *Gissel*, hundreds of organizing drives have culminated in the union being certified solely on the basis of authorization cards and without the benefit of a secret ballot election. The courts, however, have not always been hospitable to the enforcement of Board bargaining orders. See *Skyline Distribs. v. NLRB*, 99 F.3d 403 (D.C. Cir. 1996). "The courts have been strict in requiring the Board to justify *Gissel* bargaining orders, in part, because employees lose the *final say* over whether to endorse or reject unionization with the issuance of a bargaining order" (emphasis in original).

Despite the opportunities for unions to disclose the identity of card signers, the Board and some courts have held that, in the context of other unfair labor practices, it is unlawful for an employer to advise employees that cards are not confidential. However, other courts have disagreed, and since the law is unsettled in this area, caution is urged.

Nevertheless, an employer clearly has the right, indeed the obligation, to discuss the legal consequences of card execution. Employees usually are not aware of these consequences nor of the procedure for establishing the union's representative status in an unfair labor practice proceeding. Thus, it is imperative the employer inform its employees that execution of cards could authorize the union to represent them without an election. The letter reproduced as **Illustration No. 18** at pages 99 and 100, conveys this warning in language understandable to individuals unfamiliar with labor terminology or Labor Board procedure.

The employer's message in communicating with employees on this subject should correct the common "sales pitch" of union organizers that the purpose of the card is to obtain a secret ballot election; in truth, this is only one of the purposes. The language printed on the card generally controls and, more often than not, will authorize the union to represent the employees as the collective bargaining representative.

An employee may decide not to sign a card if advised that the union is engaging in deceptive solicitation practices or forcing the employee to make a premature decision concerning representation. At the very least, the employee may wish to defer a decision until he or she receives more information.

PRESENTING MANAGEMENT'S POSITION ON UNIONIZATION

How far may management go in expressing the employer's position on unions? Are there any limitations or may management say whatever will get the message across? The answers are found in NLRB and court interpretations of section 8(c) of the National Labor Relations Act, the "free speech" provision. That section preserves management's right to express opinions opposing unionization. It states:

> The expressing of any views, argument, or opinion, or the dissemination thereof, whether in written, printed, graphic, or visual form, shall not constitute or be evidence of an unfair labor practice under any of the provisions of this Act, if such expression contains no threat of reprisal or force or promise of benefit.

To the employer intent on preserving its union-free status, the expression of "views, argument, or opinion" is a requirement and not merely a statutory permit. Management must speak out forcefully, provided it does not threaten employees or promise them benefits in discouraging support for the union.

May an employer, in discussing the realities of collective bargaining, tell employees that bargaining will "start from scratch"? May an employer tell employees that the granting of union demands for increased wages and benefits may result in higher prices and less demand for its products, with adverse effects on the employees? May an employer tell employees that resistance to union demands may cause a strike, resulting in employee hardship? The answers to these and similar questions may be found in Labor Board decisions.

Bargaining Will "Start from Scratch"

This commonly used phrase has been discussed by the Board in a number of its decisions. In a leading case, the Board stated:

> Such statements are objectionable when, in context, they effectively threaten employees with the loss of existing benefits and

leave them with the impression that what they may ultimately receive depends in large measure upon what the Union can induce the employer to restore.

On the other hand, such statements are not objectionable when additional communication to the employees dispels any implication that wages and/or benefits will be reduced during the course of bargaining and establishes that any reduction in wages or benefits will occur only as a result of the normal give and take of collective bargaining. The totality of all the circumstances must be viewed to determine the effect of the statements on the employees. *Plastronics, Inc.* (1977).

The Board applied this principle to a health care employer who informed its employees in a pre-election videotape that if the union were successful, it would be "bargaining from scratch." The Board stated:

We also agree with the judge that the Respondent's "bargaining from scratch" statement merely pointed out some of the hazards and problems in collective bargaining; it was neither alleged nor argued that the Respondent threatened to take away existing benefits and restore those benefits only after a lengthy struggle in bargaining . . . . The Respondent's message to its employees that union representation was no guarantee of better benefits and might result in less desirable benefits, is legitimate campaign propaganda, which employees are capable of evaluating. Such expressions of views are protected by Sec. 8(c) of the Act. *Mediplex of Conn., Inc.* (1995).

Consequences of Negotiations

When communicating on the subject of the consequences of negotiations, a safe course is to use actual language approved by the Board, such as the following:

You should know that voting the union in does not automatically guarantee any increase in wages or other benefits, because under the law a company does not have to agree to *any* demand or proposal that a union might make. Even if it got in here, a union couldn't force us to agree to anything that we could not see our way clear to putting into effect from a business standpoint. We have just as much right under the law to ask that wages and other employee benefits be reduced as the union would have to ask that they be increased. *Fern Terrace Lodge* (1989) (emphasis in original).

The following is another example of a communication that was explicitly approved by the Board:

FACT: Only the Company can raise wages. All the Union can do is call a strike in an attempt to force the Company to do something.

FACT: By striking, a union is gambling with its members' future, hoping that it can shut off shipments to the employer's customers to gain leverage in the negotiations.

FACT: Our Company is a member of the Royal Plastics Group. If our production is interrupted in Delmont, our customers can easily be supplied from other plants, both in the United States and Canada.

FACT: Once negotiations start, all things are negotiable and wages and benefits can and often do go down because the union "trades them" for other things like a union security clause or dues check-off provision. *Custom Window Extrusions, Inc.* (1994).

Predictions Based on Objective Facts

The right of an employer to communicate to employees its views about the consequences of unionization has been addressed by the U.S. Supreme Court in *Gissel Packing Co.*, discussed earlier. There, the Court stated:

[A]n employer is free to communicate to his employees any of his general views about unionism or any of his general views about a particular union, so long as the communications do not contain a "threat of reprisal or force or promise of benefit." *He may even make a prediction as to the precise effects he believes unionization will have on his company. In such a case, however, the prediction must be carefully phrased on the basis of objective fact to convey an employer's belief as to demonstrably probable consequences beyond his control . . . .*

If there is any implication that an employer may or may not take action solely on his own initiative for reasons unrelated to economic necessities and known only to him, the statement is no longer a reasonable prediction based on available facts but a threat of retaliation based on misrepresentation and coercion, and as such without the protection of the First Amendment (emphasis added).

In other words, predictions about what might happen if the employees choose the union as their representative are permissible as long as they are based on demonstrable facts. Conversely, where the predictions are based on the employer's unsubstantiated assertions they will be held unlawful.

Cases in Point

Kawasaki Motors manufactured and sold motorcycles at its Lincoln, Nebraska, facility. A few days before a union election, the company held meetings with its employees and presented information and figures on its recent financial losses. The company stated that union work restrictions would make it difficult to operate and that it needed the flexibility to move employees from one job to another to stay competitive and survive.

The Board held that the statements were protected free speech under the *Gissel* standards. It found that Kawasaki lawfully predicted that the union's restrictive work rules would reduce the company's flexibility, threaten its profitability, and—in light of its precarious financial condition—likely push it into economic disaster. *Kawasaki Motors Mfg. Corp.* (1986).

On appeal by the union, the Ninth Circuit agreed with the Board, stating:

> The prediction about the adverse economic impact of compliance with the union's standard job classifications was based on objective circumstances beyond the company's control. Kawasaki had experience with the economic advantage of flexibility in moving its employees from one job to another. It was familiar with the problem of underutilization of labor its competitors experienced under union contracts containing rigid work rules. *A company's preelection statement about potential loss of business health due to union work restrictions is a permissible comment on possible outgrowth of unionization, not an unlawful threat.* United Auto Workers v. NLRB (9th Cir. 1987) (emphasis added).

The courts do not always agree with the Board, viewing the same facts differently, as illustrated in *Pentre Electric*. The company was engaged in the business of electrical wiring in the commercial building and construction industry. During the campaign, a co-owner told the employees that many of Pentre's customers did not employ union contractors and that, if it were unionized, the company would not have gotten the three large jobs it was presently doing. The Board upheld the union's objections to that statement on the ground that the co-owner had not provided extrinsic evidence to support the statement that Pentre customers did not use union contractors. *Pentre Elec., Inc.* (1991).

On review, the federal appeals court denied enforcement. It stated that the co-owner's statements as to the probable consequences of unionization were lawful under *Gissel*, since the statements were not subjectively phrased to convey to the employees that the company would act on its own initiative to punish its employees. Rather, the statement that its customers hired only non-union contractors was objectively phrased to refer to matters over which the company had no control. *NLRB v. Pentre Elec., Inc.* (6th Cir. 1993).

The following case graphically illustrates how closely the Board scrutinizes the language used by the employer in its communications.

Reeves Brothers was engaged in the business of dyeing and finishing fabric at its Bishopville, South Carolina, facility. Prior to an election, the company president read aloud to employees two letters from its two largest customers in which they stated that, if the union were successful, they would give strong consideration to shifting some, if not all, of their work to other non-union finishers. After reading the letters, the president stated that if the union were voted in, the customers would no longer want to do business with the company. The letters were enlarged to 8 feet x 10 feet and hung as banners from the ceiling near the entrance to the employees' canteen and posted on bulletin boards throughout the facility.

The Board set aside the election, finding that the president misrepresented the letters. The letters did not state the customers *would* take away work, only that they would *consider* doing so. Thus, the Board decided the statements went beyond the objective facts and constituted a threat of reprisal if the employees chose to be represented by the union. *Reeves Bros. Inc.* (1996).

As these cases demonstrate, there is no clear distinction between what the Board considers an objective statement of fact and what it deems a threat of reprisal. Similarly, it is often difficult in practice to distinguish between lawful argument and impermissible threat of retaliation. Generally, however, the more facts presented in support of the assertion, the more likely the prediction will be deemed to be lawful.

ILLUSTRATION NO. 15

Local Union 502

of the International Union of Electronic, Electrical, Salaried,
Machine and Furniture Workers
Affiliated with AFL-CIO
1044 Brussells Street, P.O. Box 811, St. Mary's, PA 18847

October 14, 1996

Re: Representation Election Debate

Dear Mr.   :

This will serve as an official notice that Mr. William H. Bywater, International President of the International Union of Electronic, Electrical, Salaried, Machine and Furniture Workers affiliated with AFL-CIO hereby challenges you to a debate.

Mr. William H. Bywater holds the highest office in the International Union that represents Local 502 of St. Mary's, PA. The debate will be scheduled at the Edgewood Hall off the Million Dollar Highway behind Subway on Wednesday, Ocober 16, 1996, at 6:00 P.M.

We will invite all the eligible production and maintenance employees to be present at this debate. If you do not feel comfortable taking part in this debate by yourself we invite you to bring three (3) other officials from the Company to also take part. The Union will bring Jack Shea, Director of Organization, District #1, Frank Rothweiler, International Representative and Local 502 Union President, Ed Greenawalt.

If you don't believe that the representation of the production and maintenance employee by Local 502 is not in the best interest of the workers, then you should have no problem in attending this very important debate.

Sincerely,
Frank Rothweiler
International Representative
IUE-AFL-CIO

ILLUSTRATION NO. 16

EMPLOYER RESPONSE TO UNION CHALLENGE TO DEBATE

Dear Sir:

This is in response to your letter proposing a debate between the two of us concerning the upcoming election. The company would be delighted to debate the issues with you under proper and fair conditions.

As you are well aware, the National Labor Relations Act permits you to make broad promises and statements about what the union will obtain for the employees. This same law forbids management from making any promises and drastically restricts what we can say. These restrictions place management in the position of violating the law if it discusses any plans and programs beneficial to the employees. This is why you made the offer and why we cannot accept it as proposed.

If you are sincere about a fair and honest debate, we accept your challenge. However, you must send a registered letter to us stating that, regardless of what we say in the debate, no unfair labor practice charges or objections to the election will be filed by the union.

Yours truly,

ILLUSTRATION NO. 17

EMPLOYER LETTER

UNION MISREPRESENTATIONS CONCERNING AUTHORIZATION CARDS

Dear Fellow Employee:

We have heard that a union is attempting to organize our employees. We feel very strongly that you do not need a union. We have worked very hard to provide fair working conditions for our employees. You now have good wages and fringe benefits without paying union dues or initiation fees, and without exposing yourselves to fines, assessments, and the possibility of strikes. Not one of you has lost one day's pay to get any of this.

Some of you may not be familiar with union organizing tactics. The union organizer's purpose is to get you to sign a union authorization card. YOU SHOULD BE ON YOUR GUARD!

If anyone should tell you that by signing one of these cards, you are not obligated in any way—don't believe it! This is a common trick to get people to sign cards.

Don't believe the union solicitor who states:

"This card is only to get an election or more information."

"A majority of employees have already signed."

"You must sign a card to vote."

"It will cost you more if you don't join now."

"If you don't sign now, you won't have your job after we win."

Despite what the organizers may say, signing a union card is not in your best interest.

Sincerely,

ILLUSTRATION NO. 18

EMPLOYER LETTER

LEGAL SIGNIFICANCE OF CARD SIGNING

Dear Fellow Employee:

We have recently learned that the Teamsters Union is trying to get our employees to sign authorization cards. We have drawn up a series of questions and answers to help you decide what to do.

WHAT IS AN AUTHORIZATION CARD?

It is a signed statement that an employee wants the union to be his or her collective bargaining agent.

DOES SIGNING A CARD OBLIGATE YOU?

Yes. It is a legal obligation.

WHAT MAY THE UNION DO WITH THE CARDS IT COLLECTS?

There are two possibilities:

1. If the union gets cards signed by 30 percent of our employees, it can petition the National Labor Relations Board for an election; but

2. If the union gets cards signed by a majority of our employees, it may send us a letter asking us to bargain.

IF THE UNION GETS CARDS SIGNED BY A MAJORITY AND ASKS THE COMPANY TO BARGAIN, MUST THE COMPANY DO SO?

No.

WHAT CAN THE UNION DO IF THE COMPANY REFUSES TO BARGAIN IN THESE CIRCUMSTANCES?

The union has three choices:

1. It can call an immediate strike for recognition;

2. It can request an election; *or*

3. It can give the cards to the Labor Board to count before a judge at a Board hearing.

WHAT IS THE PROCEDURE UNDER THE THIRD CHOICE?

Under this procedure, the union accuses the company of an unfair labor practice. A hearing will be held before a judge, where employees who signed cards may be called to testify. An employee may be shown his card and asked on the witness stand to identify the signature. The employee may also be questioned concerning the circumstances under which the card was signed.

If the Labor Board concludes that a majority of employees properly signed cards and that the company engaged in an unfair labor practice, it may order the company to bargain with the union, which means an election will not be held.

SHOULD YOU SIGN A CARD?

We don't think you should. Why? It legally signs away your right to choose your representative. After you have had an opportunity to learn the facts about the union, you may decide you don't want it to represent you. By signing a card now, you may be giving up your right to vote against the union if you should later change your mind.

Sincerely,

CHAPTER XII

COMMUNICATING THROUGH THE SUPERVISOR

In the employees' view, the supervisor *is* the company. Employees who respect their supervisor probably will respect their employer. Conversely, employees who dislike or distrust their supervisor will be more likely to dislike or distrust their employer, despite any generosity in wages or benefits. An informed, articulate, and respected supervisory staff is an employer's best defense against employee discontent and union incursion.

What makes one supervisor respected and another disliked? In addition to being decisive, attentive, and friendly, the good supervisor:

- Treats employees with respect and dignity;

- Investigates and resolves complaints, questions, and problems promptly and follows up;

- Enforces rules and applies policies fairly and consistently;

- Knows employees' interests, motivations, and ambitions;

- Listens and encourages ideas and suggestions; and

- Keeps employees informed of departmental and company-wide changes, accomplishments, and goals.

THE LEGAL STATUS OF THE SUPERVISOR

Supervisors are not "employees" under the Act and their right to organize is not protected. The Act's definition of a supervisor and the criteria for determining supervisory status are discussed in Chapter XV at page 150.

Occasionally, a supervisor will encourage employees to join a union. As the employer's agent, a supervisor's support of the union may indicate employer support, which is a violation of section 8(a)(2) of the Act. That section makes it an unfair labor practice for an employer to "dominate or interfere with the formation or administration of any labor organization or contribute financial or other support to it."

A supervisor who supports the union should be directed to cease such activity and may be disciplined or terminated. However, an employer may not discipline the supervisor if the supervisor refuses to commit an unfair labor practice, files a charge against the company, or gives testimony adverse to company interests.

TRAINING SUPERVISORS IN THEIR RESPONSIBILITIES

Supervisory training in good management and communication practices is an essential part of a preventive employee relations program and is the key to an employer's union-free status. Supervisors should be trained to recognize and resolve legitimate employee needs. If not addressed, even small irritations can fester into major problems. The supervisor's prompt attention to employee complaints will help avoid this and will show employees that they need not go outside the organization for assistance.

Supervisors should recognize employee unrest and union interest and relay this information to an appropriate company official. There are many signs that a union organizing campaign may be starting:

- Employees meet and talk in out-of-the-way places and separate when the supervisor approaches them;
- Employee complaints increase or the nature of the complaints change;
- Complaints are made by a delegation, rather than by a single employee;
- Employees adopt a new vocabulary that includes such phrases as "security," "dignity," and "justice;"
- Employees ask argumentative questions more frequently and aggressively in departmental meetings;
- News items about union settlements in local companies or other industries appear on company bulletin boards;
- Graffiti appears expressing hostility toward supervisors or the company;
- Employees who used to talk openly to supervisors have stopped doing so;
- Employees who appear to have little in common form new friendships;

- Employees are visited at their homes by union agents; and

- Union authorization cards or leaflets are found on the premises or in parking areas.

Supervisors should not underestimate these signs and should "over-communicate" rather than "under-communicate" to whom they report concerning these indicia of union interest.

Supervisors must understand and appreciate the company's legitimate reasons supporting its philosophy concerning unions and should be trained how and when to communicate this philosophy to employees. They should know that they are expected to discuss the prospect of unionization with their employees openly, accurately, lawfully, and assertively.

Some employers fail to encourage supervisors to take this approach during the early stages of an organizing campaign. As a result, employees may be unaware of all the disadvantages, costs, and risks of union representation and may be swayed by the union organizer's sales pitch.

To encourage their participation in management's efforts against organizing, supervisors should understand the consequences a unionized facility would have upon them. Often they will be restricted in their ability to manage and direct the work force and hamstrung by shop stewards in their relations with employees. Management should use these facts to motivate supervisors to talk to employees concerning unionization.

TRAINING SUPERVISORS IN THEIR RIGHT OF FREE SPEECH

Supervisors have the same statutory right as any other company official to express their "views, argument, and opinion" concerning the undesirability of unions and unionization. They may speak out freely against unions, as long as they do not threaten employees with unlawful retaliation or promise them special benefits. For example, a supervisor may tell employees:

- "The company and I are opposed to unionization;"

- "You do not have to sign a union card;"

- "You do not have to speak to union organizers or admit them into your home;"

- "With a union you may have to take your problems to a shop steward instead of dealing directly with me;"

- "Union membership costs a lot—you would have to pay dues and initiation fees and face the possibility of fines and assessments;"

- "The union's strike record is terrible; it's another risk you would face if the union gets in." (The supervisor may not, however, state that a strike is inevitable in the event of unionization);

- "If a union calls you out on an economic strike, you may be permanently replaced and would be reinstated only when and if an opening occurs;" and

- "Union negotiations are an uncertain process; you may get more, it could be the same, or you may wind up with even less than what you have now."

Supervisors should be encouraged to initiate conversations with employees on these points and show a willingness to answer questions. They do not have to know all the answers, but they must follow-up with the correct information.

TRAINING SUPERVISORS TO AVOID UNLAWFUL STATEMENTS

Another important element of a supervisor's communications training is instruction concerning potentially unlawful statements. The basic prohibitions can be remembered by using the acronym "T I P S":

T   *Threats*: Do not threaten employees with unlawful company action to cause them to refrain from union activities.

I   *Interrogation:* Do not question employees about their union sentiments or activities.

P   *Promises:* Do not promise special, unplanned benefits.

S   *Surveillance:* Do not spy on employees' union activities or give the impression of doing so.

Specifically, supervisors should be instructed *not* to:

- Promise employees pay increases, promotions, improved working conditions, additional benefits, or special favors on condition that the employees not support the union;

- Threaten employees with plant closure, loss of job, or reduction in wages in retaliation for supporting the union;

- Tell employees they would have received a wage increase but for the start of the union campaign;

- Tell employees that there will be a strike if the union is successful (although recounting the *possibility* of a union strike is permitted);

- Discriminate against an employee participating in union activities by separating him or her from other employees;

- Equate union activity with disloyalty to the employer;

- Discipline an employee for soliciting another employee to sign an authorization card when both are on non-working time;

- Question employees about their opinion or that of other employees concerning the union, union activities, internal union affairs, union meetings, or whether they have signed a union card;

- Call an employee into a management office to discuss the union; or

- Visit employees at their homes on a systematic basis to urge them to reject the union.

Typical Employee Questions

The following are some typical questions employees ask of their supervisors and some suggested lawful responses.

(a) Authorization Cards

Q. Do I have to let a union representative into my house?

A. No. A union representative has no more right than any other door-to-door salesperson to enter your house.

Q. Do I have to sign an authorization card?

A. No. You don't have to sign anything to work here.

Q. What difference does it make if I sign a card?

A. By signing a card, you may be giving up your right to vote in an election. Under certain circumstances, the government could order the company to bargain with the union based on these cards.

Q. But the union says they need cards for an election; is this so?

A. While they can use cards to request an election, they can also use these cards to demand recognition, call you out on a recognitional strike, or request the government to order the company to bargain, *without an election.*

Q. If I sign one of these cards, can I get it back?

A. You can write to the union asking for the card back, but it is unlikely you will get it.

(b) Costs to Employee

Q. Will it cost me anything to belong to this union?

A. Yes. Members commit to pay dues every month, initiation fees, and possibly fines and extra assessments.

Q. What can the union fine me for?

A. The union can fine you for a variety of reasons—for example, not attending union meetings, coming into work if there is a strike, or talking back to an officer of the union.

Q. How can the union force me to pay these fines?

A. Union fines are considered legal debts. If you don't or can't pay up, the union can take you into court and get a judge to order you to pay.

(c) Negotiations

Q. Won't it mean more money for me if the union gets in?

A. No, not necessarily. The union *cannot guarantee* any wage increase or benefit improvement.

Q. If the union wins an election, will the company automatically have to agree to the union's demands?

A. No, the company does not have to agree to any demand that it feels is not good business and might be harmful to the company.

Q. Won't a union insure my job security?

A. No. The way an employee's job security can be insured is your company continuing to grow and remaining competitive with other companies in its industry. Your job security is in doing a good job.

(d) Strikes

Q. What happens if the company and the union don't agree?

A. The union can call you on strike.

Q. If the union calls a strike, can I be replaced?

A. Yes, the law allows the company to hire new employees to permanently replace economic strikers.

Q. If the union calls us out on strike, what happens to my regular pay and benefits?

A. While on strike, your pay stops and you would have to pay the whole monthly premium to keep your health insurance going.

Q. If the union calls me out on strike, will the union pay me anything?

A. Most unions require walking the picket-line to receive strike benefits.

It is lawful to discuss the hardship of strikes as one of the possible consequences of unionization, as long as the supervisor refrains from leading the employees to believe strikes are "inevitable." In one decision, the Board stated:

> In outlining the advantages and disadvantages of unionization, an employer is not prohibited from pointing out that the strike is a union's chief economic lever, and that strike action might entail certain consequences. But the more the employer persists in referring to strikes and what they might entail—replacement, violence, unemployment, walking picket lines, unpaid bills—the more the employee is likely to believe that the employer has already determined to adopt an intransigent bargaining stance which will force employees to strike in order to gain any benefits.

> An employer who campaigns on the theory that a strike is an inevitable result of unionization leaves himself open to the construction that he does not intend to bargain in any meaningful sense. *Thomas Prods. Co.* (1967).

Answering Questions About a Scheduled Wage Increase

Employees often are concerned about the effect an election petition may have on a scheduled wage increase. They want to know if the increase will take place. Should the union lose the election, the wrong answer to this question can mean a rerun election ordered by the Labor Board.

When instructing supervisors how to respond, it is important to keep in mind the Labor Board's general rule: an employer is required to proceed with an expected wage or benefit adjustment as if the union was not on the scene.

An employer may postpone such an adjustment if it makes it clear the adjustment will occur whether or not the employees select a union and as long as the sole purpose of the delay is to avoid the appearance of influencing the election's outcome. Supervisors answering employees' questions about a postponement must be careful to avoid creating the impression the union stands in the way of the planned increase.

Cases in Point

● A few weeks before a scheduled election, a company wrote to its employees:

> Many of you have asked what the company is going to do about a pay raise in January. I regret to notify you that the January adjustments in wage rates and benefits will have to be postponed for all employees involved in the pending NLRB Election.

> This delay is required to avoid the appearance of vote-buying by the company in view of the fact that the NLRB will hold an election on January 8. Our counsel has advised us that wage

increases at this time might be considered to be an unfair labor practice and that the company should not take this risk.

An employee then asked his supervisor why there would be no increase. The supervisor replied it was because of the union campaign. The Board held that, while the statements in the letter were lawful, the supervisor's reply blaming the union for the postponement was not. The Board ordered a second election. *Atlantic Forest Prods.* (1987).

● A union filed a petition to represent pharmacists employed by a supermarket chain. The company sought advice about salary increases from its counsel who responded:

> We have reviewed your Salary Administration Program, past and present, and advise that, if the Guild were to file an unfair labor practice charge, or an objection to the election based upon the increases given after May 27, the date of the petition, there is a good possibility the NLRB would hold the increases unlawful or set aside the election. The safest course would be to suspend the increases until after the election. The Board has approved this approach, providing the employer makes clear that the purpose in doing so is to avoid the appearance of election interference.

The company wrote to the pharmacists, paraphrasing the counsel's letter and advising them it was suspending salary reviews until after the election. Later, the company's director of pharmacy held a meeting with the pharmacists to advise them reviews had been suspended because it might be unlawful to continue them with the election pending.

The union filed charges that the suspension was unlawful. At the hearing, three employees testified that the pharmacy director had said the suspension "was because of the union business." Although the director denied this, the administrative law judge ordered the company to restore the suspended increases retroactively with interest. The Board affirmed. *Borman's Inc.* (1989).

The suspension of wage increases while objections to an election or challenges to ballots are pending is discussed in Chapter XIX at page 216.

TRAINING SUPERVISORS TO RESPOND TO UNION COMMUNICATIONS

Illustration No. 19 at page 111, is an example of a typical union handbill. It boldly asserts "Only Through Unionization Do Workers Receive *Justice On The Job*," listing among other benefits, "guaranteed wage increases," "seniority rights," and "grievance rights." Early in the campaign, and preferably before the union openly communicates with the employees, supervisors should be trained to anticipate and answer this commonly used union propaganda. With this early training, supervisors can more readily respond to the union's communications when they are received.

When the actual propaganda is distributed, the message should be analyzed for any inaccurate, incomplete, or misleading statements in a short briefing session. Management officials then should discuss the appropriate response with the supervisors who, in turn, will convey it to the employees in their own words. This way supervisors become active participants in management's counter-campaign.

Guaranteed Wage Increases

The union's promise of guaranteed wage increases may sound appealing, but the union cannot guarantee anything. In fact, as with all terms and conditions of employment, wage rates may even decrease as a result of good faith bargaining. The supervisor may state that the employer will continue its progressive wage and benefit practices, pursuant to which employees have received increases and benefits without payment of union dues.

Seniority Rights

Unions find the concept of seniority recognition and its benefits easy to sell since employees generally agree that job security should increase with length of service. The supervisor may remind the employees that the employer has a long-standing policy to consider length of service in layoffs, recall from layoffs, transfers, and promotions as well as certain personnel policies, such as vacation preferences. However, less senior but highly motivated employees may suffer disadvantages if the emphasis on seniority affects advancement opportunities.

Grievance Rights

The union's promise of an opportunity to voice complaints and challenge adverse personnel decisions through a formal grievance and arbitration procedure (see **Illustration No. 20** at page 112) has appeal unless the employer has adopted and promoted some alternative format to resolve workplace issues such as one or more of the established alternative dispute resolution procedures discussed in Chapter IV.

Written Contract

A major part of the union's pitch is the assurance of a binding, written contract. The supervisor may respond by referring to the company's employee handbook containing its personnel policies. The supervisor may assert that a union contract often provides rigid and inflexible procedures restricting an employer from taking the steps that may be necessary to avoid a business failure. There are many examples of unionized companies that have not survived in the face of competitive pressures. The former employees of such companies may have "enjoyed" a union contract, but they ended up having no place to enjoy it.

Unionism and Job Security

A standard union claim is that unionization brings "job security." This phrase is a catchword that creates an emotional appeal. It implies employees are guaranteed perpetual employment. Deflating the union's promise of job security can be troublesome. To attack it may suggest the employee's job is tenuous and create fears of termination or layoff. This trap may be avoided by explaining what job security really is: being hired by and working for a healthy, growing company with the reasonable assurance of steady work. It is the employer, not the union, who provides this. More specifically, job security is:

- Having a place to work;

- Having equipment with which to work;

- Having no interruptions in work;

- Getting paid every pay day; and

- Enjoying vacations and holidays with pay and having a job to come back to afterwards.

The supervisor should explain these concepts when responding to the union's claim that it provides "job security." The union's emotional appeal may be further deflated by pointing out that a union contract does not guarantee permanency of employment. No union contract can guarantee employment if a business fails, if there is a seasonable drop-off in sales, or if a lengthy strike causes a loss of customers.

A union can do little to enhance a company's success, but it can do much to prevent it. Unreasonable demands, slowdowns, strikes, spurious grievances, and opposition to improved methods of production all hurt a company's ability to operate efficiently and make a profit. A company that is not profitable does not remain in business.

Face to face interaction between supervisors and employees complement the employer's other methods of communication. If instructed properly, supervisors can effectively influence employee attitudes and opinions and enhance the level of trust and credibility enjoyed by the employer.

ILLUSTRATION NO. 19

UNION HANDBILL

JUSTICE . . .
ON THE JOB!

ONLY THROUGH UNIONIZATION DO WORKERS RECEIVE JUSTICE ON THE JOB!

YOU TOO CAN RECEIVE THE FOLLOWING BENEFITS, WHICH THOUSANDS OF

LOCAL 888 MEMBERS ENJOY:

* GUARANTEED WAGE INCREASES
* SENIORITY RIGHTS
* MAJOR MEDICAL
* HOSPITALIZATION
* DENTAL COVERAGE
* OPTICAL COVERAGE
* PAID SICK LEAVE
* PRESCRIPTION COVERAGE
* LIFE INSURANCE
* GRIEVANCE RIGHTS
* JURY DUTY PAY
* BEREAVEMENT PAY
* PAID VACATIONS

SIGN AND MAIL THE ATTACHED UNION CARD...FOR JUSTICE ON THE JOB...
FOR ALL

LOCAL 888
U.F.C.W. - A.F.L.C.I.O.

ONE WESTCHESTER TOWER
100 EAST FIRST STREET
MT. VERNON, NY   10550

ILLUSTRATION NO. 20

WHEN YOU HAVE A GRIEVANCE

SEE YOUR STEWARD
(or your district committeeperson)
WHO TALKS TO THE SUPERVISOR

IF UNSETTLED
YOUR COMMITTEEPERSON
NEGOTIATES WITH SUPERVISOR

IF STILL UNSETTLED
THE SHOP COMMITTEE
TAKES IT TO TOP MANAGEMENT

THEN IF NEEDED
WE ARBITRATE
WITH HELP FROM
THE INTERNATIONAL UNION REPRESENTATIVE

CHAPTER XIII

RESPONDING TO THE UNION'S DEMAND FOR RECOGNITION

Weeks go by—perhaps months—while union talk circulates on and off the employer's premises. One day the employer receives a letter or personal visit from a union representative claiming to represent a majority of the employees and demanding the employer recognize the union as their bargaining agent. **Illustration No. 21** at page 118 is an example of a demand for recognition letter.

Most unions as a matter of policy will not request recognition unless they have procured signed authorization cards from a majority of the employees. Why do unions follow this course?

First, if recognition is granted, the ensuing bargaining relationship will be lawful because it is founded on majority status, a requirement under the Act. Second, if recognition is not granted and the union files a petition for an election, the union's possession of a majority of cards will enhance its likelihood of success in the election. Third, if a demand for recognition is rejected and the employer subsequently commits serious unfair labor practices, the union's possession of cards from a majority of employees will better enable it to seek a remedial bargaining order from the Board. See discussion of *Gissell Packing Co., Inc.* (U.S. 1968) in Chapter XI at page 90.

REJECTING CARD CHECKS

If the employer refuses recognition, the union representative may offer to prove its claim of majority support by a card check. A card check is a comparison of signatures on authorization cards with signatures on the company's payroll records. The union representative may ask that the employer make the comparison in the representative's presence or that it be made by a disinterested third party.

Caught off guard, and without knowing the consequences, a company official might unwittingly agree to a card check. The actual comparison may demonstrate that the union possesses cards from a majority of the employees. If the employer then reneges on its agreement, the Labor Board will order the employer to recognize and bargain with the union. However, looking at the cards, without agreeing to be bound by the results, will not alone afford *de facto* recognition. *Trevose Family Shoe Store* (1978).

To avoid a Board order to bargain, a union's offer to prove majority representation by a card check should be rejected. The reasons are clear: (1) If the employer accepts the offer and the comparison of signatures demonstrates the union has majority support, the Board may direct the employer to recognize and bargain with the union without an election; (2) If the comparison demonstrates that the union does not have a majority, the employer has gained nothing. The union only resumes its campaign and returns another day with more cards.

DECLINING RECOGNITION

An employer may lawfully decline to recognize and bargain with a labor organization upon receiving a demand for recognition and need not give any reason for its refusal. Therefore, a union's demand for recognition based solely on its claim that it has a majority of employees "signed up" should be rejected. There are cogent reasons for doing so. First, the union may not in fact have majority support in an appropriate unit. Recognition of a minority union by an employer is unlawful. Second, the cards on which the union bases its claim may be invalid for the following reasons:

- The signatures may have been forged. See, for example, *Imco Container Co.* (1964) and *Drug Fair-Community Drug Co., Inc.* (1967).

- The signatures may have been obtained through coercion. Employees may have been threatened that unless they signed they would be out of a job once the union got in.

- The cards may be stale, that is, invalid because of the passage of time. Generally, cards are valid for a period of one year.

- The cards may be ambiguous or dual-purpose cards which authorize a union to file a petition for an election or support a demand for recognition. See, for example, **Illustration No. 22** at page 119.

- The cards may be clear and unambiguous, but the language on the cards may have been superseded by the misleading talk of the solicitors (discussed below).

- The cards may have been revoked (discussed below).

- The cards may have been tainted by supervisory assistance (discussed below).

These reasons should put an employer on guard against the hasty acceptance of a union's demand for recognition based on signed authorization cards. Generally, an employer has nothing to gain and everything to lose by agreeing to recognition based upon cards. The employer should respond by insisting on a secret ballot election (see **Illustration No. 23** at page 120 for an example of a response) and then communicate the union's request and its response to the employees.

Misrepresentations as to the Purpose of the Card

It is not uncommon for union organizers to make misleading statements to employees concerning the purpose of authorization cards, such as the card will only be used to obtain an election when in fact it is used in support of a demand for recognition.

When employees are told that obtaining an election is "one" of the purposes of a card, the signed card may be counted in determining majority status. However, the card will not be counted if the employee was told that the *sole, single,* or *only* purpose of the card is to obtain an election. *NLRB v. Gissel Packing Co., Inc.* (U.S. 1968).

Revoked Cards

An employer may on its own initiative inform employees of their right to revoke signed union authorization cards. The employer may communicate the procedure for revoking the cards by bulletin board notice, letter, speech, or individual conversation, providing the employer does not monitor the results or create a situation where employees "would tend to feel peril in refraining from such revocation." *R.L. White Co., Inc.* (1982). Beyond providing information on the procedure for revoking cards, an employer may render only limited ministerial assistance such as providing the union's address. If the assistance becomes more than ministerial, it may be unlawful.

No formality is required for an employee to revoke a card. It may be accomplished by a letter to the union or by a statement to the individual who initially solicited the signature. The only requirement is a simple, clear, and unambiguous declaration that the employee no longer wishes to be represented by the union and wants the card returned.

Cards validly revoked by employees prior to the company's receipt of a demand for recognition will generally not be counted in establishing the union's majority status. However, they may be counted in determining the union's 30% showing of interest to support an election petition.

Supervisory Taint

An employer may refuse to recognize a union if supervisory assistance was used to obtain signed cards. Cards are tainted when supervisors encourage signing or otherwise render improper assistance. The Board has refused to permit these "tainted" cards to be used to show majority support for the union. Similarly, "tainted" cards may not be used by a union to support the 30% showing of interest required to file a petition.

POLLING EMPLOYEES

Some employers react to a union's claim that it represents a majority of employees by polling the employees for verification. Although it is permissible for a union to conduct a poll of employees, such a poll by an employer is unlawful unless handled carefully.

The Board has permitted such polls by employers only when (1) the purpose of the poll is to determine the truth of a union's claim of majority status, (2) this purpose is communicated to the employees, (3) assurances against reprisal are given, (4) the employees are polled by secret ballot, and (5) the employer has not engaged in unfair labor practices or otherwise created a coercive atmosphere. *Struksnes Constr. Co., Inc.* (1967).

The Labor Board tolerates little deviation from these rules and in most cases has held that the employer failed to satisfy these criteria. Another important reason to be cautious about polling is the possibility that it may result in a confirmation of the union's majority claim and subject the employer to a Board order to recognize and bargain with the union.

UNLAWFUL RECOGNITION—SWEETHEART CONTRACTS

Although most unions will not demand recognition without majority support, occasionally a union with less than a majority or without any employee authorization will make a demand. An agreement executed under these circumstances is called a "sweetheart contract" or "top-down deal." An employer's agreement to such an arrangement is unlawful and a minority union that enters into such a contract with an employer is equally guilty. (Section 8(f) of the Act provides an exception for employers and unions in the construction industry and allows them to enter into collective bargaining agreements even though the union does not enjoy majority status.)

The contract is open to attack by employees or by another union. If the contract provides for compulsory union membership or checkoff, the employer may be held liable for losses incurred by employees forced to pay union dues and initiation fees. The employer is not relieved of liability by claiming it mistakenly believed the union represented a majority of the employees.

Employers who sign "sweetheart contracts" or contracts with "easy to live with" minority unions are deceiving themselves. Even if no one blows the whistle, these arrangements pose an ever present threat that someday the "friendly" union may affiliate with or be displaced by a more militant union.

UNION RESPONSE TO EMPLOYER'S REFUSAL OF RECOGNITION

A union that has been refused recognition has the burden of invoking the Board's election procedure. If the union has not already done so, it will file a petition for an election, thus initiating the final phase of the campaign. In many instances, the union will file a petition with the NLRB simultaneously with its demand for recognition and seek to persuade a majority of employees to support it in a Board conducted election. However, increasingly unions are mounting corporate campaigns (discussed in Chapter IX) to coerce the employer's recognition. See Steven Greenhouse, *Unions, Bruised in Direct Battles with Companies, Try a Roundabout Tactic, The New York Times,* March 10, 1997, at B7.

Occasionally, a union will seek to force an employer to recognize it by picketing its place of business. Should the employer succumb, recognition of the union would be involuntary and may be without employee assent. Such recognition is subject to attack as unlawful due to lack of majority representation.

An employer confronted with recognitional picketing may file an unfair labor practice charge against the union and file a petition for an election as discussed in the following chapter. The employer's objective is to obtain an expedited election and a certification by the regional director that a majority of employees do not wish to be represented by the union. If the union pickets after having lost an election, the employer may then charge the union with unlawful picketing for recognition within twelve months of a valid election.

ILLUSTRATION NO. 21

OCAW

Oil, Chemical & Atomic Workers
International Union, AFL-CIO

INTERNATIONAL REPRESENTATIVE
JOHN BARCELLONA
71 HIGH STREET
WOODBRIDGE, NJ 07095
PHONE   (908) 636-7343

JULY 5, 1996

DEAR _____,

ON BEHALF OF THE PRODUCTION, MAINTENANCE & SHIP-
PING AND RECEIVING EMPLOYEES AT _____
BETHLEHEM, PA. AND THE OIL, CHEMICAL & ATOMIC
WORKERS INTERNATIONAL UNION, AFL-CIO, AND PURSUANT
TO THE NATIONAL LABOR RELATIONS ACT, I AM HEREWITH
NOTIFYING AND SERVING UPON YOU A TRUE COPY OF A
PETITION, SIGNED BY THE MAJORITY OF THE PRODUCTION,
MAINTENANCE, & SHIPPING AND RECEIVING EMPLOYEES
DEMANDING THAT YOU RECOGNIZE THE OIL, CHEMICAL &
ATOMIC WORKERS INTERNATIONAL UNION AS THEIR SOLE
AND EXCLUSIVE BARGAINING AGENT.

IN CONJUNCTION WITH THIS PETITION, THE OCAWIU
HEREWITH DEMANDS THAT YOU RECOGNIZE US AS THE
SOLE AND EXCLUSIVE REPRESENTATIVES ON BEHALF OF
SAID EMPLOYEES FOR THE PURPOSES OF COLLECTIVE
BARGAINING IN REGARDS TO WAGES, HOURS, AND ANY AND
ALL OTHER CONDITIONS OF EMPLOYMENT.

YOU ARE REQUIRED BY LAW TO REFRAIN FROM
BARGAINING OR ENTERING INTO CONTRACTUAL RELATIONS
WITH ANY OTHER LABOR ORGANIZATION.

SINCERELY,

ILLUSTRATION NO. 22

CONFIDENTIAL
AUTHORIZATION CARD

Authorization for Representation
Under the National Labor Relations Act

YES, I WANT THE IAM

I, the undersigned employee of

(Company)

authorize the International Association of Machinists and Aerospace Workers (IAM) to act as my collective bargaining agent for wages, hours and working conditions. I agree that this card may be used either to support a demand for recognition or an NLRB election, at the discretion of the union.

Name (print) _____ Date _____

Home Address _____ Phone _____

City _____ State _____ Zip _____

Job Title _____ Dept. _____ Shift _____ Plant _____

Sign Here x _____

NOTE: This authorization to be SIGNED and DATED in Employee's own handwriting. YOUR RIGHT TO SIGN THIS CARD IS PROTECTED BY FEDERAL LAW.

ILLUSTRATION NO. 23

Employer Response to Union Demand for Recognition

This is in reply to your letter in which you state that a majority of our employees have authorized your union to represent them and in which you request that we recognize your union. We do not believe you represent an uncoerced and informed majority of our employees in an appropriate unit. Therefore, we reject your request that we recognize and bargain with your union.

Your offer to establish proof of your majority by a card check is unacceptable. A mechanical check of signatures would not resolve whether an employee was coerced into signing a card or whether he or she signed a card as a result of misrepresentation as to its purpose. We believe, as does the United States Supreme Court, that a secret ballot election is the best way to determine whether a union has majority support. Therefore, if you have a sufficient number of cards signed by our employees, we suggest you file a petition for an election with the National Labor Relations Board.

Yours truly,

General Manager

PART III

WINNING THE ELECTION

CHAPTER XIV

PETITIONING THE LABOR BOARD

Anticipating employers will refuse their request for recognition, many unions simultaneously file a petition for certification with the NLRB. To understand the procedure in filing a petition, it is helpful first to examine the Labor Board's administrative structure.

There are thirty-three regional offices. Each regional office is headed by a regional director who is appointed by the Board on recommendation of the General Counsel. The office also employs supervisory personnel, field attorneys, field examiners, and non-professional employees.

FILING AN ELECTION PETITION

Petitions are filed with the regional director for the region in which the bargaining unit is located. An original and four copies are required. The regional office will supply the necessary form (see **Illustration No. 24** at page 134), which may be used for a number of other purposes (see Item 1, Purpose of This Petition).

LABOR ORGANIZATION AS PETITIONER

The most frequently filed petition is for Certification of Representative filed by a labor organization. The petitioner alleges that a substantial number of employees wish to be represented for purposes of collective bargaining and that the petitioner desires to be certified as their representative (see **Illustration No. 24** at page 134, Item 1, first box, "RC—Certification of Representative").

The petitioner must allege and submit proof that the petition is supported by 30% or more of the employees in the alleged appropriate bargaining unit (see **Illustration No. 24** at page 135, Item 6(b)). Such proof must be presented when the petition is filed or within forty-eight hours thereafter and is almost always in the form of dated executed authorization cards. Occasionally, it may take another form such as a petition signed by the required number of employees. Unions will sometimes use this approach to show solicited employees that their peers had previously signed.

Item 7a of the petition form asks for the date the petitioner requested and was denied recognition. It should be noted, however, that a demand for recognition is not required before filing the petition.

Occasionally, two or more unions are "joint petitioners." The two unions appear on the ballot as a single entrant and, if successful in the election, they will be certified jointly. If the unions later want to abandon this joint relationship and bargain separately, the employer may insist they bargain together.

An intervening union needs only one signed authorization card to get its name on the ballot with the petitioning union. An intervening union which demonstrates support of at least 10% of the employees in the appropriate bargaining unit may become a full participant in the representation process and will have the same rights as the petitioning union in deciding election matters. Regardless of the number of unions on the ballot, the winning union needs a majority of the votes cast by employees in the appropriate bargaining unit.

Upon the filing of the petition, the regional director sends the employer a "Notice of Representation Hearing," notifying it that a petition has been filed and enclosing a copy of the petition (see **Illustration No. 25** at page 136). Lately, regional directors have telefaxed this notification and copy of the petition to employers, in addition to mailing it by registered mail, so as to accelerate the administrative process.

Usually the employer then contacts an attorney who will enter an appearance. All further documents and correspondence will be served on the attorney as well as the employer. If counsel prefers to receive exclusive service, the employer must execute and file NLRB Form 4813 "Notice of Designation of Representative as Agent for Service of Documents" (see **Illustration No. 26** at page 137).

When the employer receives notice of the petition, it also receives a "Notice to Employees" for posting (see **Illustration No. 27** at page 138). There is no obligation to post this notice and the employer may decide not to since it contains examples of employer misconduct. The employer may post its own notice that a petition has been filed as a way of establishing itself as the source of information about the election.

INVESTIGATING THE PETITION

The regional director will investigate whether a question concerning representation ("QCR") exists. He or she will determine: whether the employer's business is in interstate commerce or affects commerce; whether the petitioned for unit is appropriate; whether the petitioner has submitted proof of authorization from at least 30% of the employees in the unit requested; and whether there is a written collective bargaining agreement in effect barring the filing of the petition.

The regional director's investigation is administrative in nature. Issues involving fraud, forgery, coercion, revocation, or supervisory taint of the cards should be raised during the investigation since they may not be litigated at a formal hearing. *Crystal Art Gallery* (1997).

When the regional director notifies the employer that a petition has been filed the director asks the employer to complete a "Commerce Questionnaire" (see **Illustration No. 28** at page 139). This enables the regional director to make a finding that the employer is engaged in interstate commerce within the meaning of the Act. There is no penalty for not returning the questionnaire.

Any labor dispute occurring in interstate commerce is subject to the National Labor Relations Act and the jurisdiction of the Labor Board. Even when a business is not engaged in interstate commerce, it may be subject to NLRB jurisdiction if its operations "affect commerce." Thus, the Board may assert jurisdiction over even a purely local business if a labor dispute interrupting its operations could have an impact on the flow of commerce.

The Board's statutory jurisdiction, as described above, should be distinguished from its discretionary jurisdiction. On its own initiative, the Board has taken jurisdiction of universities, the U.S. postal service, profit making hospitals, nursing homes, agencies of foreign governments, and law and accounting firms. In deciding to assert jurisdiction in a particular case, the Board follows self-imposed industry standards based upon a minimum dollar volume of business. These guidelines, well within the Board's statutory jurisdiction, are discretionary.

When the regional director notifies the employer that a petition has been filed, the director also requests an alphabetized list of employees' names and job classifications to verify the adequacy of the union's "showing of interest," i.e. that the union has submitted authorization cards from at least 30% of the employees in the unit requested. (See **Illustration No. 28** at page 139).

Should an employer comply with this request and submit a list? This often depends upon whether it plans to challenge the union's showing of interest. Some employers are reluctant to submit the list, believing the union may gain access to it. It also may be undesirable at that point to commit to the inclusion or exclusion of certain employees from the unit.

On the other hand, there may be a good reason to submit a list. If the union has understated the number of employees in the unit, it may be unable to demonstrate support from at least 30% of the actual number of employees in the unit. In this event, the employer should seriously consider submitting the list and requesting dismissal of the petition.

In the usual case there is no cause for dismissing the petition and the regional director goes forward with the investigation. However, if the regional director finds that a QCR does not exist, the director may request the petitioner to withdraw its petition. If the petitioner refuses, the director will dismiss it, stating the ground for dismissal. The petitioner may then appeal to the Labor Board in Washington.

EMPLOYER PETITIONS

A petition filed by an employer is commonly known as an RM ("representation-management") petition. An RM petition alleges that one or more individuals or labor organizations has presented a claim for recognition as the employees' representative. It may be filed in various situations.

Union Request for Recognition Without Accompanying Petition for Election

In the preceding chapter, we discussed the union's request for recognition and the employer's response. When an employer declines recognition, it has the right to file a petition to resolve the union's claim, but it has no obligation to do so.

The petition form is the same one used by unions. (See **Illustration No. 24** at page 134). The employer checks the second box in Item 1, "RM—Representation (Employer Petition)," alleging that "one or more individuals or labor organizations have presented a claim to petitioner (the employer) to be recognized as the representative of employees of Petitioner."

When completing the petition, counsel should consider whether the bargaining unit claimed by the union to be appropriate is in fact appropriate. If counsel merely recites the unit as stated in the union's demand, the employer may be conceding the appropriateness of the bargaining unit claimed by the union.

The RM petition should be accompanied by proof of the union's request for recognition, such as an affidavit reciting an oral request. If the union's request was made in writing, a copy of the letter should be attached. Such proof must be submitted within forty-eight hours after the petition has been filed; otherwise, the petition may be dismissed.

Employer Doubt of Union's Continued Majority Status

If an employer has been unable to reach an initial agreement with a newly certified union and has a reasonable doubt based on objective considerations that the union has lost its majority status, it may file a petition for a new election. The petition is not timely until one year after the date of the union's certification.

An employer also may file a petition when it doubts the majority status of a union with which it has a contract. The petition is timely if filed between the 90th and 60th day before the contract expires (in the health care industry, the "open period" is between the 120th or 90th day prior to the contract's expiration) or after the contract has expired and before a new agreement has been executed. The petition must be supported by objective proof that the labor organization has lost its majority status. An assumption of lost majority based on an apparent lack of interest or activity in the bargaining unit is not enough. The proof must be objective and direct, rather than subjective and circumstantial.

An employer who doubts an incumbent union's continued majority support does not have to file a petition; it may withdraw recognition during the period when a petition may be filed. The Board has stated:

[A]n employer may lawfully withdraw recognition from an incumbent union because of an asserted doubt of the union's continued majority if its assertion of doubt is raised in a context free of unfair labor practices and is supported by a showing of objective considerations providing reasonable grounds for a belief that a majority of the employees no longer desire union representation. *Southern Wipers, Inc.* (1971).

Where the withdrawal occurs during the contract, the union must be permitted to continue to administer the contract until its expiration.

Even if the employer has filed a timely petition, the union may seek to block it by filing an unfair labor practice charge. The employer's petition then is held in abeyance while the Labor Board investigates the charge. Unions often use this strategy when they doubt they can win the election requested by the employer's petition.

If the union wants the regional director to continue to process the representation case notwithstanding the charge, it will execute a "Request to Proceed," stipulating that it will not file objections based upon conduct that occurred prior to filing the petition. The representation case and the investigation of the unfair labor practice charge will then proceed simultaneously. However, when the charge alleges that the company is refusing to bargain in good faith [section 8(a)(5)], the representation proceeding may be stayed until a determination is made with respect to the merits of the charge.

To defend a refusal to bargain charge, the employer must submit evidence that the union in fact no longer enjoys majority status or that the withdrawal of recognition was based on a reasonable doubt as to the union's continued majority status. The doubt must be based on objective considerations and raised in a context free of employer unfair labor practices.

Examples of objective considerations that may support an employer's doubt of continuing majority status include:

- an admission by the union that it no longer represents a majority of the employees;

- a request by a majority of employees to discontinue bargaining;

- unambiguous statements by unit employees that they no longer desire union representation;

- a petition by a majority of unit employees rejecting continued representation;

- significant changes in bargaining unit personnel during a strike; and

- a downward trend in the number of employees authorizing dues deductions.

The employer has a third option where it doubts majority support. Prior to filing a petition or withdrawing recognition, it may poll its employees to assess the degree of waning support for the union. However, in order to lawfully conduct the poll, the employer's doubt of the union's majority status must be based on objective considerations that the union's support has fallen below a majority. In addition, the polling process must adhere to the Board's procedural guidelines discussed in Chapter XIII. See *Allentown Mack Sales and Serv., Inc. v. NLRB* (D.C. Cir. 1996), *cert. granted* (U.S. 1997).

A decertification petition (discussed next) cannot serve as the basis for a withdrawal of recognition since the petition only requires the signatures of 30% of bargaining unit employees. Although the petition may have the support of a majority of employees, the Labor Board as a matter of policy does not disclose this information to the employer. One appellate court has suggested that as a defense to a refusal to bargain charge the employer should formally request this information. *NLRB v. New Assocs.* (3d Cir. 1994).

DECERTIFICATION PETITIONS

Where employees question the need for continued union representation either because employers develop improved work environments or for other reasons, the National Labor Relations Act guarantees employees the right to decertify a union through a Board-conducted election. While a part of the law since 1947, decertification is a well-kept secret about which there is little published information. Yet, between 1980 and 1995, employees have decertified unions in 8,421 collective bargaining units.

Filing Procedure

A decertification petition may be filed by an employee, a group of employees, or any individual or organization acting on their behalf. The decertification petition must be supported by 30% of the employees in the certified or recognized bargaining unit. The third box in Item 1 of the petition form entitled "RD Decertification" must be checked (see **Illustration No. 24** at page 134).

If no contract has been negotiated, a decertification petition may be filed any time after the expiration of one year from the date of a union's certification. If there is an existing contract, a petition may be filed only during the "open periods" discussed earlier or after the contract has expired and before a new one is executed.

When a decertification petition is filed, the NLRB regional office will notify the employer and request a list of employees to verify the petitioner's claim of 30% support among the employees in the unit. The regional director will then schedule a conference and seek the parties' consent to an election.

Absent agreement, a hearing will be ordered to decide any outstanding issues. Typically, the union raises issues such as employee eligibility, the appropriateness of the unit, or the timeliness of the petition. After the hearing, the regional director will review the record, decide the issues, and direct an election or dismiss the petition. The election is held among employees in the certified unit or the unit as described in the collective bargaining agreement according to Board procedures concerning representation elections.

The Employer's Contract Obligations

The filing of a decertification petition during a contract's "open period" does not allow an employer to suspend negotiations or withdraw recognition. On its face, the petition indicates nothing more than the disaffection of 30% of the employees in the bargaining unit. The employer must continue to abide by all the terms of the contract until it expires and, upon request, engage in negotiations, unless the employer has objective evidence of the union's lack of majority status. If no agreement is reached and the contract expires, the employer must continue to abide by its terms and conditions, except for the dues check-off and union security provisions, until negotiations have reached an impasse.

An employer's legal obligation toward the union is significantly changed once it knows that a decertification or employee petition is supported by a *majority* of employees. Then, the employer may assert a "good faith" doubt that the union continues to have majority support and suspend bargaining for a new contract.

Under these circumstances, the employer's right to withdraw from *bargaining* prior to the contract's expiration does not create a collateral right to withdraw *recognition*. A union has the right to continue to administer the contract until it expires. After the contract expires, it is lawful to withdraw recognition as well as withdraw from bargaining based upon a good faith doubt of the union's majority status. At that point, the employer unilaterally may implement changes in benefits and conditions of employment.

The Employer's Role

An employer has limited rights to assist employees in ousting their union. The Board's longstanding rule is that an employer may not initiate, instigate, solicit, encourage, or assist employees in filing a decertification petition. Where an employer "plants" the idea to decertify in its employees' minds through unsolicited advice or provides more than ministerial aid, the petition is "tainted" and the employer's actions are unlawful.

Cases in Point

The service department employees at an automobile dealership in Missouri were represented by the International Association of Machinists. After the contract had expired, one of the employees asked the service manager for assistance in typing the language on an employee petition to evidence interest in decertifying the union. At the manager's request, one of the office clerks typed the petition on the company's letterhead and returned it to the manager, who left it on his desk for several days. After it was signed by most of the employees, the manager asked the employee to file it with the Labor Board.

The Board held that the company's involvement in the decertification effort was unlawful. By permitting the petition to be circulated on company letterhead, allowing it to remain on the manager's desk, and asking the employee to forward it to the NLRB, the employer had unlawfully assisted the employees. *Placke Toyota, Inc.* (1974).

Similarly, in *Vic Koenig Chevrolet, Inc.* (1996), the Board held an employer provided more than ministerial aid when it furnished clerical help, the use of a copy machine, corrected the language of a decertification petition, and arranged for an attorney to verify signatures on the petition using company personnel files.

Conversely, if an employer provides "mere ministerial aid" to the decertification effort, its action does not taint the decertification effort. For example, where an employee asks a manager how to remove the union, the manager may lawfully respond by informing the employee about the mechanics of decertification and furnish the Board's regional office address and telephone number.

Case in Point

Eastern States Optical Company sold and distributed eyeglass lenses and frames in New York. Its employees were represented by the Warehouse Production Sales and Service Employees Union. An order clerk who wanted to oust the union phoned the company's attorney and informed him the employees were seeking to decertify the union. The clerk also asked about how to word the caption on an employee petition.

At the attorney's suggestion, the clerk contacted the NLRB regional office and obtained a decertification petition form. When he had trouble completing it, he phoned the attorney again for the description of the bargaining unit and the number of employees. After getting the signatures of a majority of the employees, the clerk mailed the petition to the company, which withdrew recognition from the union.

The union filed charges. The Board held that the attorney's actions did not rise to the level of unlawful assistance and concluded that the company's withdrawal of recognition was lawful. It noted the company had played no role in the clerk's decision to initiate the decertification proceedings, the employee was the one who initiated the two contacts with the attorney, and the attorney did not say anything to encourage or facilitate the petition. *Eastern States Optical Co.* (1985).

The Employer's Campaign

Contrary to popular belief, it is lawful for an employer to take an active role in campaigning to decertify a union after a petition has been filed. An employer may campaign as vigorously as it would in resisting the initial organization.

The employer's strategy should emphasize employees would be better off without the union and they have everything to gain and nothing to lose. The employer must be prepared to respond to union arguments that, absent representation, employees will lose seniority rights and union-secured wages and benefits, assuring employees they will not lose anything they currently enjoy under the contract if the union is decertified. A promise to maintain the status quo is lawful.

Election Procedure

The procedure in conducting a decertification election is the same as a certification election. The incumbent union must receive a majority of the votes to retain its certification. A tie vote results in decertification.

It is noteworthy that, where decertification was attempted over the past 15 years, unions lost 72.6% of the elections in which they participated.

DEAUTHORIZATION PETITIONS

Another less frequently used petition is the deauthorization petition (see **Illustration No. 24** at page 134, fourth box of Item 1, "UD—Withdrawal of Union Shop Authority"). It may be filed when at least 30% of the bargaining unit employees want to rescind the union security provision of their collective bargaining agreement. The voting unit must be coextensive with the contractual unit.

As with a decertification petition, the employer may not sponsor or assist in its preparation. Unlike a decertification petition, however, a deauthorization petition may be filed at any time during the term of an existing contract, even within twelve months of a certification election.

A majority of the employees in the bargaining unit (not a majority of those voting, as in other elections) must vote in favor of rescinding the security clause. The union's status as the employees' bargaining agent is unaffected by a favorable vote and the contract continues in all other respects for the balance of its term. The practical result is that employees have no obligation to join the union and pay dues; however, the labor organization still represents all unit employees regardless of their membership.

UNIT CLARIFICATION PETITIONS

An employer or a union may file a petition for unit clarification when there is a dispute about whether certain employees should be in the bargaining unit (see **Illustration No. 24** at page 134, Item 1, box 5). No vote is held; the Board decides whether the employees should be part of the unit.

A unit clarification petition may be filed by an employer to determine, for example, whether particular employees are supervisors and should be removed from the bargaining unit. It also may be filed by a union seeking to enlarge the unit it represents. If the union is successful, the employees are added without an opportunity to vote on whether they want the union to represent them. For this reason, the Board disfavors such a result. Generally, it will not allow this "accretion" to take place if the employees sought to be added are themselves part of a group that could constitute a separate appropriate unit. *Safeway Stores, Inc.* (1981).

AMENDMENT OF CERTIFICATION PETITIONS

A petition to amend an existing certification (see **Illustration No. 24** at page 134, Item 1, box 6) may be filed by an employer or a union to reflect a change in circumstances, such as a different name or affiliation of the union or name or location of the employer. Again, no vote is held. The Board makes the decision.

To enhance its ability to win an NLRB election, an employer must have knowledge of the mechanics of processing a representation petition. This subject will be discussed in the next chapter.

ILLUSTRATION NO. 24

FORM NLRB-502
(5-85)

FORM EXEMPT UNDER 44 U S C 3512

UNITED STATES GOVERNMENT
NATIONAL LABOR RELATIONS BOARD
PETITION

DO NOT WRITE IN THIS SPACE

Case No.	Date Filed

INSTRUCTIONS: Submit an original and 4 copies of this Petition to the NLRB Regional Office in the Region in which the employer concerned is located. If more space is required for any one item, attach additional sheets, numbering item accordingly.

The Petitioner alleges that the following circumstances exist and requests that the National Labor Relations Board proceed under its proper authority pursuant to Section 9 of the National Labor Relations Act.

1. PURPOSE OF THIS PETITION (If box RC, RM, or RD is checked and a charge under Section 8(b)(7) of the Act has been filed involving the Employer named herein, the statement following the description of the type of petition shall not be deemed made.) **(Check One)**

☐ **RC-CERTIFICATION OF REPRESENTATIVE** - A substantial number of employees wish to be represented for purposes of collective bargaining by Petitioner and Petitioner desires to be certified as representative of the employees.

☐ **RM-REPRESENTATION (EMPLOYER PETITION)** - One or more individuals or labor organizations have presented a claim to Petitioner to be recognized as the representative of employees of Petitioner.

☐ **RD-DECERTIFICATION** - A substantial number of employees assert that the certified or currently recognized bargaining representative is no longer their representative.

☐ **UD-WITHDRAWAL OF UNION SHOP AUTHORITY** - Thirty percent (30%) or more of employees in a bargaining unit covered by an agreement between their employer and a labor organization desire that such authority be rescinded.

☐ **UC-UNIT CLARIFICATION** - A labor organization is currently recognized by Employer, but Petitioner seeks clarification of placement of certain employees: (Check one) ☐ In unit not previously certified. ☐ In unit previously certified in Case No. _____ .

☐ **AC-AMENDMENT OF CERTIFICATION** - Petitioner seeks amendment of certification issued in Case No. _____
Attach statement describing the specific amendment sought.

2. Name of Employer	Employer Representative to contact	Telephone Number

3. Address(es) of Establishment(s) involved (Street and number, city, State, ZIP code)

4a. Type of Establishment (Factory, mine, wholesaler, etc.)	4b. Identify principal product or service

5. Unit Involved (In UC petition, describe **present** bargaining unit and attach description of proposed clarification.)	6a. Number of Employees in Unit:
Included	Present
	Proposed (By UC/AC)

ILLUSTRATION NO. 24 (CONT.)

Excluded

6b. Is this petition supported by 30% or more of the employees in the unit? * _____ Yes _____ No
*Not applicable in RM, UC, and AC

(If you have checked box RC in 1 above, check and complete EITHER item 7a or 7b, whichever is applicable)

7a. ☐ Request for recognition as Bargaining Representative was made on *(Date)* _____ and Employer declined recognition on or about *(Date)* _____ *(If no reply received, so state).*

7b. ☐ Petitioner is currently recognized as Bargaining Representative and desires certification under the Act.

8. Name of Recognized or Certified Bargaining Agent *(If none, so state)* | Affiliation

Address and Telephone Number | Date of Recognition or Certification

9. Expiration Date of Current Contract, If any *(Month, Day, Year)*

10. If you have checked box UD in 1 above, show here the date of execution of agreement granting union shop *(Month, Day, and Year)*

11a. Is there now a strike or picketing at the Employer's establishment(s)? _____ Yes _____ No
11b. If so, approximately how many employees are participating? _____

11c. The Employer has been picketed by or on behalf of *(Insert Name)* _____ , a labor organization, of *(Insert Address)* _____ Since *(Month, Day, Year)* _____

12. Organizations or individuals other than Petitioner *(and other than those named in items 8 and 11c)*, which have claimed recognition as representatives and other organizations and individuals known to have a representative interest in any employees in unit described in item 5 above. *(If none, so state)*

Name	Affiliation	Address	Date of Claim *(Required only if Petition is filed by Employer)*

I declare that I have read the above petition and that the statements are true to the best of my knowledge and belief.

_____ *(Name of Petitioner and Affiliation, if any)*

By _____ _____
(Signature of Representative or person filing petition) *(Title, if any)*

Address _____ _____
(Street and number, city, State, and ZIP Code) *(Telephone Number)*

WILLFUL FALSE STATEMENTS ON THIS PETITION CAN BE PUNISHED BY FINE AND IMPRISONMENT (U. S. CODE, TITLE 18, SECTION 1001)

ILLUSTRATION NO. 25

FORM NLRB 852
(7-82)

UNITED STATES OF AMERICA
BEFORE THE NATIONAL LABOR RELATIONS BOARD

Employer

CASE

Petitioner

NOTICE OF REPRESENTATION HEARING

The Petitioner, above named, having heretofore filed a Petition pursuant to Section 9(c) of the National Labor Relations Act, as amended, 29 U.S.C. Sec. 151 et seq., copy of which Petition is hereto attached, and it appearing that a question affecting commerce has arisen concerning the representation of employees described by such Petition.

YOU ARE HEREBY NOTIFIED that, pursuant to Sections 3(b) and 9(c) of the Act, on June 7, 1996 at 10:00 a.m., and on consecutive days thereafter, at the Thomas P. O'Neill, Jr. Federal Building, 10 Causeway Street, Sixth Floor, Boston, Massachusetts, a hearing will be conducted before a hearing officer of the National Labor Relations Board upon the question of representation affecting commerce which has arisen, at which time and place the parties will have the right to appear in person, or otherwise, and give testimony. (Form NLRB-4669, Statement of Standard Procedures in Formal Hearings Held Before The National Labor Relations Board Pursuant to Petitions Filed Under Section 9 of The National Labor Relations Act, as Amended, is attached.)

Signed at Boston, Massachusetts on the 24th day of May, 1996.

/s/ Rosemary Pye
Regional Director, Region One
National Labor Relations Board

ILLUSTRATION NO. 26

FORM NLRB-4813
(11-64)

National Labor Relations Board

**NOTICE OF DESIGNATION OF REPRESENTATIVE
AS AGENT FOR SERVICE OF DOCUMENTS**

CASE NO.

TO: Regional Director,

I, the undersigned party, hereby designate my representative, whose name and address appear below and who has entered an appearance on my behalf in this proceeding, as my agent to receive exclusive service of all documents and written communications relating to this proceeding, including complaints and decisions and orders, but not including charges, amended charges, subpoenas, directions of elections or notices of elections, and I authorize the National Labor Relations Board to serve all such documents only on said representative. This designation shall remain valid until a written revocation of it, signed by me, is filed with the Board.

Full name of party	Representative's name, address, zip code (print or type)
Signature of party (please sign in ink)	
Title	
Date	Area Code Telephone Number

ILLUSTRATION NO. 27

NOTICE TO EMPLOYEES

FROM THE
National Labor Relations Board

A PETITION has been filed with this Federal agency seeking an election to determine whether certain employees want to be represented by a union.

The case is being investigated and NO DETERMINATION HAS BEEN MADE AT THIS TIME by the National Labor Relations Board. IF an election is held Notices of Election will be posted giving complete details for voting.

It was suggested that your employer post this notice so the National Labor Relations Board ~ould inform you of your basic rights under the National Labor Relations Act.

YOU HAVE THE RIGHT under Federal Law

- To self-organization
- To form, join, or assist labor organizations
- To bargain collectively through representatives of your own choosing
- To act together for the purposes of collective bargaining or other mutual aid or protection
- To refuse to do any or all of these things unless the union and employer, in a state where such agreements are permitted, enter into a lawful union-security agreement requiring employees to pay periodic dues and initiation fees. Nonmembers who inform the union that they object to the use of their payments for nonrepresentational purposes may be required to pay only their share of the union's costs of representational activities (such as collective bargaining, contract administration, and grievance adjustments).

It is possible that some of you will be voting in an employee representation election as a result of the request for an election having been filed. While NO DETERMINATION HAS BEEN MADE AT THIS TIME, in the event an election is held, the NATIONAL LABOR RELATIONS BOARD wants all eligible voters to be familiar with their rights under the law IF it holds an election.

The Board applies rules that are intended to keep its elections fair and honest and that result in a free choice. If agents of either unions or employers act in such a way as to interfere with your right to a free election, the election can be set aside by the Board. Where appropriate the Board provides other remedies, such as reinstatement for employees fired for exercising their rights, including backpay from the party responsible for their discharge.

NOTE:

The following are examples of conduct that interfere with the rights of employees and may result in the setting aside of the election.

- Threatening loss of jobs or benefits by an employer or a union
- Promising or granting promotions, pay raises, or other benefits to influence an employee's vote by a party capable of carrying out such promises
- An employer firing employees to discourage or encourage union activity or a union causing them to be fired to encourage union activity
- Making campaign speeches to assembled groups of employees on company time within the 24-hour period before the election
- Incitement by either an employer or a union of racial or religious prejudice by inflammatory appeals
- Threatening physical force or violence to employees by a union or an employer to influence their votes

Please be assured that IF AN ELECTION IS HELD every effort will be made to protect you right to a free choice under the law. Improper conduct will not be permitted. All parties are expected to cooperate fully with this Agency in maintaining basic principles of a fair election a required by law. The National Labor Relations Board, as an agency of the United State Government, does not endorse any choice in the election.

NATIONAL LABOR RELATIONS BOARD

an agency of the

UNITED STATES GOVERNMENT

ILLUSTRATION NO. 28

United States Government
NATIONAL LABOR RELATIONS BOARD
Region 1 Boston, Massachusetts
10 Causeway Street, 6th Floor
Boston, MA 02222-1072
(617) 565-6700

May 24, 1996

Dear Sir or Madam:

I am enclosing a copy of a Petition that has been filed with this office. The National Labor Relations Board has developed procedures to expedite representation cases. This letter and the enclosed materials describe those basic procedures.

The Board agent named below will explore the issues with the parties and attempt to obtain an election agreement. If no election agreement is reached, the Board agent may conduct an informal conference either at the Regional office or by telephone, prior to the date of the scheduled formal hearing. At this conference, the Board agent will make further efforts to obtain an election agreement or, at least, narrow the issues that will be litigated at the hearing. These informal conferences can be extremely useful in helping to explore potential areas of agreement to eliminate, or limit to the extent possible, the significant costs of litigation.

To assist us in our investigation, please submit the following information immediately:

1.   Commerce information, which may be furnished on the enclosed "Questionnaire on Commerce Information," Form NLRB-5081.

2.   For the payroll period immediately preceeding the date of this letter, an alphabetized list of employees described in the petition and their job classifications. This list will help determine the scope of the unit and the voter eligibility of various classifications or individuals and determine the adequacy of the Petitioner's showing of employee interest to conduct an election.

3. Copies of correspondence and existing or recently expired contracts, if any, covering employees in the unit alleged in the petition. Names of any other labor organization(s) claiming to represent any of the employees in the proposed unit.

4. Your position as to the appropriateness of the unit.

When you provide the list of employees and their classificatons, I strongly encourage you to authorize the Board agent assigned to the case to release this information to the other parties to aid the resolution of the issues.

In addition to the list of employees you provide initially, if an election is ultimately scheduled, the employer must file a list of the full names and addresses of all the eligible voters, the *Excelsior* list, within 7 days of the direction of election or approval of an agreement to conduct an election.

If the initial processing and conference call do not result in an election agreement, an NLRB Hearing Officer will hold a formal hearing in this case. To ensure an early date for such a hearing, I enclose the Notice of Hearing directing that the hearing be conducted on June 7, 1996. Requests for a change of the hearing date must comply with the requirements set forth in Form NLRB-4338, which is enclosed. The hearing will be conducted on consecutive work days until completed, unless the most compelling circumstances warrant otherwise.

You have the right to be represented by counsel or other representative in any proceeding before the National Labor Relations Board. If you choose to have a representative appear on your behalf, please have your representative complete "Notice of Appearance," Form NLRB-4701. If you want any representative to exclusively receive all documents mailed by this office in this case, you must complete the "Notice of Designation of Representative as Agent for Service of Documents," Form NLRB-4813. Both forms should be returned to this office as soon as possible. In the event you exercise your right to be represented by counsel or other representative, you should do so promptly, as a delay by a party in seeking representation will not warrant a postponement of the hearing on the date set forth above.

If you or your representative intend to file a post-hearing brief, you can make arrangements with the reporting-service contractor to obtain the transcript on an expedited basis. If you do not request expedited delivery, a request for an extension of time to file a brief based upon a delay in the delivery of the transcript will be denied.

If an election is scheduled, you will receive copies of the Board's Official Notice of Election. I am alerting you now to Board Rule 103.20, which is enclosed, describing the procedures for posting the Board's Official Notice of Election. Failure to comply with this rule is grounds for setting aside the election, if proper and timely objections are filed.

When a petition such as this one is filed, employees may have questions about what is going on and what may happen. To address these questions, please post the enclosed Notice to Employees in conspicuous places in areas where employees such as those described in the enclosed petition work. Copies of this notice are also being made available to the labor organization(s) involved. In addition, I am enclosing two copies of the pamphlet "Your Government Conducts an Election," for distribution to employees and to supervisory personnel. Additional copies of the pamphlet will be furnished upon request.

Under the Freedom of Information Act, representation petitions are subject to prompt disclosure to members of the public. Therefore, you may have received or may receive a solicitation by organizations or persons who have obtained public information and seek to represent you before our Agency. Be assured that no organization or person seeking your business has any "inside knowledge" or favored relationship with the National Labor Relations Board; their information regarding this matter is only that which must be made available to any member of the public.

The Board agent assigned to your case will be able to answer any additional questions. Your cooperation in this matter is appreciated.

Very truly yours,

/s/Rosemary Pye

Rosemary Pye
Regional Director

Enclosures:

Petition

Notice to Employees

The National Labor Relations Board and You: Representation Cases

Your Government Conducts an Election

NLRB Rule 103.20

NLRB Forms 852, 4338, 4701, 4812, 4813, and 5081

Board Agent: Joan M. Healey, Senior Election Specialist,
Telephone No.: 617-565-6756

CHAPTER XV

PROCESSING THE REPRESENTATION PETITION

As discussed in the preceding chapter, immediately after the union files a petition for representation, the agency's regional director will notify the employer and enclose a "Notice of Representation Hearing," designating a hearing date within two weeks after the petition is filed.

ELECTION AGREEMENTS

Prior to the date of the hearing, the Board agent assigned to the case will phone the parties and explore their positions concerning the appropriate bargaining unit, the supervisory status of employees, and voter eligibility in an attempt to reach an agreement on these issues. If there are no disagreements, he will seek to have them enter into a "Stipulated Election Agreement." (See **Illustration No. 29** at page 158). By executing this agreement, the parties waive their right to a hearing to determine the bargaining unit and agree that the Board, rather than the regional director, shall determine all questions relating to the election, such as challenged ballots or objections.

It is well-settled Board policy that a Stipulated Election Agreement is a binding contract to which the parties will be held and that if the unit description of that agreement is expressed in clear and unambiguous terms, the Board will not examine extrinsic evidence to determine the parties' intent regarding bargaining unit composition. *Laidlaw Transit, Inc.* (1997).

If the parties can reach agreement on the unit, it is sometimes advisable to enter into a side agreement listing the names of all employees who will be included in the unit and thus eligible to vote, rather than simply defining the unit in general terms. This is permitted under the Board's decision in *Norris-Thermador Corp.* (1958). Such an agreement (not surprisingly called a "Norris Thermador agreement") normally will minimize the possibility of challenged ballots and subsequent litigation.

An employee whose name is listed cannot be challenged as ineligible to vote, unless the employee's status contravenes either the National Labor Relations Act or established Board policy. For example, as the Act prohibits the parties from including supervisors in the bargaining unit, either party could challenge a voter whom it claimed was a supervisor, despite the appearance of that person's name on a *Norris Thermador* agreement. An employee whose name is not listed will not be eligible to vote.

A party may withdraw from an election agreement any time before the regional director has approved it. After the regional director's approval, a party may withdraw only upon an affirmative showing of unusual circumstances or if all parties agree.

SELECTING THE DATE OF ELECTION

Choosing the optimum election date is a decision that must be weighed carefully. Should an employer seek an early date on the theory that the union will not have time to "sell" its employees or because of a gut feeling that "its people" will not let it down? Or should it seek to avail itself of the normal time allowed by the Board's procedures? Currently, most regional directors will not approve an election agreement setting an election date more than 49 days from the date on which the petition is filed.

An employer's decision to expedite the election is usually unwise. By the time a petition is filed, the union has already been making its sales pitch for several weeks or months and the employer may have done little or nothing. On the day of the conference the union's strength is probably at its zenith.

Only when an employer is convinced that the union will be rejected should it agree to an early election date. Few employers can be so certain of the outcome of the election. An employer should, therefore, seek an election date that provides as much time as is necessary to furnish employees with sufficient facts to make an informed decision.

THE HEARING

If the parties are unable or unwilling to enter into an election agreement, a formal hearing will be held. Section 9(c)(1) of the Act provides for an "appropriate" preelection hearing when a petition is filed seeking a representation election if the Board upon investigation has reasonable cause to believe that a question concerning representation affecting commerce exists. See *Barre-National, Inc.* (1995); *Angelica Healthcare Servs. Group, Inc.* (1995).

Unions often seek to have their employee supporters attend the hearing for strategic reasons. Generally, if a union feels it necessary to have employees present it will subpoena them. An employer may not discipline an employee for complying with a Board subpoena. *Yenkin-Majestic Paint Corp.* (1996). Board procedures for revoking subpoenas must be followed.

When subpoenas are not issued, the regional director engages in a balancing test, weighing the employees' interests in attending the proceeding against the employer's interests in maintaining production and discipline over the work force. Each case is determined on its individual facts. Employers should discuss the situation with counsel before considering disciplining employees for attending a Board hearing.

A representation hearing is considered non-adversarial in nature. The rules of evidence used in federal and state courts are not controlling. The hearing officer, however, is instructed to follow such rules whenever possible.

After opening the hearing, the hearing officer will ask counsel or other party representatives to note their appearances and inquire whether there is any other labor organization in the hearing room claiming an interest in the proceeding or wishing to intervene. When another labor organization is present, it will normally make a formal motion to intervene. The proposed intervenor must state the basis for its assertion that it has an interest in the proceeding. Its claim may be based upon a contract covering all or part of the employees in the proposed unit or its possession of at least one authorization card.

STIPULATIONS

Shortly after the opening of the hearing, the parties will be asked to stipulate that the employer is engaged in interstate commerce. If the parties cannot so stipulate, it becomes a contested issue on which testimony will be taken.

In most cases, the commerce question is not an issue. However, in order to assert jurisdiction, a "commerce finding" must be included by the regional director in his or her decision. Rather than submit detailed testimony, the parties may stipulate for the record that the employer meets the Board's jurisdictional standards. The employer's actual business volume need not be stated.

The parties will also be asked to stipulate that the petitioner is a labor organization. On occasion, counsel will refuse to do so because he or she is unfamiliar with the particular local union or because of a serious question as to its legal standing. The petitioner then must prove that it satisfies the elements of a "labor organization" as defined in the NLRA:

> The term "labor organization" means any organization of any kind, or any agency or employee representation committee or plan, in which employees participate and which exists for the purpose, in whole or in part, of dealing with employers concerning grievances, labor disputes, wages, rates of pay, hours of employment, or conditions of work.

This definition of labor organization has been construed very broadly by the Board and the courts, and it is rare that a union will not meet the standard. A claim that a union is not genuine because it is dominated or controlled by the employer cannot be raised at this hearing, as it alleges an unfair labor practice which may not be litigated in a representation proceeding.

Next, the hearing officer will inquire, "Does the company decline at this time to recognize the petitioner as the exclusive bargaining agent for the employees in the unit petitioned for until such time as it is certified as such in the appropriate unit determined by the Board?" If the company responds affirmatively, the hearing officer will incorporate the question and answer into a stipulation. A *note of caution*: The Board has sometimes used such answers in representation hearings as evidence of a refusal to bargain in a subsequent unfair labor practice proceeding. The employer may be well advised, therefore, to decline to answer this question.

The major task of the hearing officer is to insure that a complete record is made. Since the employer generally has possession of the facts relevant to the issues, a management official normally will be the first and, possibly, the only witness.

CLOSING THE HEARING

After the testimony is presented, the hearing officer will ask the union whether it is willing to participate in an election in any unit found appropriate. This is an important question that is often overlooked. If the union answers in the negative and the regional director finds a voting unit different from that requested by the union, the regional director will dismiss the petition.

The hearing officer will then inquire whether any party wishes to file a brief. It is advisable to do so, as a brief provides the employer an opportunity to cite prior Board decisions supporting its position and generally argue its case.

The Board's rules provide that briefs are due within seven days. It is usually necessary to request an extension of time. The hearing officer may grant such an extension not to exceed fourteen additional days. If the hearing officer refuses to grant such an extension, it then becomes necessary to request an extension in writing from the regional director after the hearing closes. The hearing officer's role ends after the close of the hearing. He or she does not make recommendations to the regional director concerning resolution of the issues.

DETERMINING THE APPROPRIATE UNIT

After the hearing is closed and briefs are filed, the entire record is reviewed by the regional director or a designee. Their major responsibility is to determine the appropriate unit.

The NLRA sets forth alternative bargaining units from which the regional director may choose. It may be the employer's entire establishment, a craft, a single plant, or a subdivision of a plant. Section 9(c)(5) of the Act prohibits the regional director, when determining whether a particular unit is appropriate, from giving controlling weight to the extent to which the employees have been organized by the union. For example, the employer may have shown at the hearing that the union sought to represent only assembly line employees in a factory and made no effort to organize other production workers. In the case of a retail chain, the employer may have demonstrated that the union confined its organizing to only one of several stores. This type of evidence may be considered by the regional director, provided it is not a controlling factor in deciding the appropriate unit issue.

The NLRA does not state the indicia for including or excluding employees from a voting unit or specify what is an "appropriate unit." It merely empowers the Board to decide the question in each case. Thus, the regional director has wide discretion in determining appropriate units and is not required, in making the decision, to find the most appropriate unit. He or she is only required to find *an* appropriate unit.

The Board recently reviewed the principles underlining its determination of "appropriate" units:

> In deciding the appropriate unit, the Board first considers the union's petition and whether that unit is appropriate. The Board, however, does not compel a petitioner to seek any particular appropriate unit. The Board's declared policy is to consider only whether the unit requested is an appropriate one, even though it may not be the optimum or most appropriate unit for collective bargaining. "There is nothing in the statute which requires that the unit for bargaining be the *only* appropriate unit, or the *ultimate* unit, or the *most* appropriate unit; the Act only requires that the unit be 'appropriate.'" *Overnite Transp. Co.* (1996) (internal citations omitted).

To make a unit determination the regional director weighs all the factors relevant to the "community of interest" of the employees. Among the factors considered in determining whether employees have a sufficient community of interest with other employees to mandate their inclusion or exclusion in the same voting unit are similarities or differences in:

- Hours of work;
- Job duties;
- Compensation;
- Rest periods and lunch hours;
- Holidays, vacations, pensions, and insurance;
- Employee facilities;
- Production methods;
- Tools, equipment, and skills;
- Overall supervision; and
- Permanent or temporary transfers between departments and facilities.

The greater the similarities in the above factors among groups or classifications of employees, the more likely they will be included in the same voting unit. When the exclusion of an employee or classification of employees is sought, evidence should be presented demonstrating a dissimilarity of working conditions and other factors in order to establish the absence of a community of interest.

The statute's definition of employee excludes agricultural laborers, domestic servants, individuals employed by a parent or spouse, independent contractors, supervisors, and anyone employed by an employer subject to the Railway Labor Act or by an employer who is not covered by the NLRA.

The Board is forbidden from finding appropriate a bargaining unit that groups guards and other employees together or that includes professional with nonprofessional employees, unless a majority of the professional employees vote expressly for such inclusion.

Employee inclusion and exclusion is the subject of thousands of Board decisions. While there are many classifications of employees that may be disputed in a Board representation proceeding, the following list covers those classifications most often in issue:

(1) *Part-time employees*—Part-time employees are included in a unit provided they perform work within the unit on a regular basis for a sufficient period of time. Although each case is determined on its own facts, employees who work at least four

hours per week on a regular basis generally will be eligible to vote as regular part-time employees.

(2) *On-call employees*—The inclusion of this classification of employees is dependent on whether there is a pattern of regular, continuing employment and a substantial probability of continued employment.

(3) *Seasonal employees*—The key factor in determining whether seasonal employees are included in a bargaining unit is whether they have a reasonable expectation of reemployment. The Board looks at the employer's rehiring policies. If the employer gives preference to former employees or has a recall policy or practice with respect to its seasonal employees, the Board will generally include seasonal employees in the voting unit.

(4) *Students*—Students are included in the voting unit provided they meet the same general criteria as regular employees or regular part-time employees. Thus, if they perform unit work on a regular basis over a sufficient period of time, for pay, they will be included. Students hired as summer employees must meet the criteria of seasonal employees to be included in the voting unit.

(5) *Trainees*—The inclusion of these employees is based on an evaluation of their current interests and duties in relation to those of the other employees in the voting unit, rather than their prospective assignment upon completion of the training.

(6) *Dual-function employees*—Employees who perform bargaining unit work during some of their working time are included in the voting unit if they meet the standards set forth for part-time employees.

(7) *Confidential employees*—The Board excludes confidential employees from voting units. Confidential employees, as defined by the Board, are persons who assist and act in a confidential capacity to persons who formulate, determine, and effectuate management policies in the field of labor relations.

(8) *Managerial employees*—Managerial employees are excluded from voting units. Managerial employees are those who formulate, determine, and effectuate management policies and who have discretion in performing their jobs.

(9) *Office and plant clerical employees*—As a general rule, the Board excludes office clerical employees from units of production employees, unless a community of interest can be demonstrated between these groups of employees. It should be noted, however, that office clerical employees who do not share such a

relationship with production employees can, by themselves, constitute an appropriate voting unit. Plant clerical employees who have a close working relationship with production employees are usually included in a unit of production employees.

Supervisory Status

The most litigated issue in representation cases is whether an individual is an eligible employee or a supervisor who is excluded from the bargaining unit. Whether a person is a supervisor depends upon whether his or her responsibilities satisfy the NLRA's definition.

Section 2(11) of the Act defines a supervisor as:

any individual having authority, in the interest of the employer, to hire, transfer, suspend, lay off, recall, promote, discharge, assign, reward, or discipline other employees, or responsibly to direct them, or to adjust their grievances, or effectively to recommend such action, if in connection with the foregoing the exercise of such authority is not of a merely routine or clerical nature, but requires the use of independent judgment.

The authority to exercise or "effectively to recommend" any of these actions, combined with independent judgment, establishes supervisory status, since the definition is read in the disjunctive.

When initiating an inquiry as to the supervisory status of an individual, an employer should examine whether the individual, in the interest of the employer:

- Assigns work;
- Directs employees;
- Grants time off;
- Evaluates work;
- Schedules work hours;
- Recommends or executes discipline;
- Hires and fires employees;
- Receives a salary;
- Receives higher pay than other employees;
- Interviews job applicants;
- Keeps workers' time records;
- Consults with management on production problems;
- Authorizes overtime and selects employees for overtime;
- Has authority to adjust grievances;
- Participates in a profit sharing plan;

- Attends supervisory meetings; or
- Exercises independent judgment in carrying out asserted "supervisory" activities.

The exercise of independent judgment is the crucial factor in determining supervisory authority. For example, if work is assigned to an employee merely on the basis of the machine the employee operates, the individual assigning the work would not be exercising independent judgment and thus would not possess supervisory authority. The assignment would be merely routine. If, however, the assignment of work could have been made to one of several employees and the individual who assigned the work did so on the basis of the employee's skill, that assignment of work would not be routine and would demonstrate the exercise of independent judgment. The individual assigning the work would be a supervisor under the Act.

Cases in Point

A circuit court of appeals held, contrary to the Board, that a grocery store night manager exercised independent judgment by calling the police and evacuating the store upon receiving an anonymous bomb threat. The court stated: "The fact that an employee responds to emergencies by exercising independent judgment rather than awaiting orders from supervisors is indicative of supervisory status." *Schnuck Markets, Inc. v. NLRB* (8th Cir. 1992).

In two leading cases, the Board held that hospital charge nurses and licensed practical nurses were not supervisors because in performing their duties they lacked independent judgment and acted in a routine or clerical nature in coordinating the patient care within their areas. See *Providence Hosp.* (1996); *Ten Broeck Commons* (1996).

Practical Considerations

There are certain supervisors in every company who clearly are a part of management. However, there may be other employees whose eligibility to vote is borderline. An employer must seriously ponder the inclusion or exclusion of these employees. If they are included in the unit and the union wins the election, they will be covered by the contract. On the other hand, some elections are lost by only a few votes. With the benefit of hindsight, the employer who has lost a close election may regret the day caution influenced it to exclude these employees from the voting unit.

REQUEST FOR REVIEW

Upon completion of a review of the record, the regional director will set forth the unit determination in a decision and direction of election. A party who disagrees with the regional director's decision may request review by the Board in Washington, D.C. within fourteen days after service of the decision. The other party may file a statement in opposition to the request for review. The Board will grant review only upon one or more of the following grounds:

1. A substantial question of law or policy is raised because of (a) the absence of, or (b) a departure from, officially reported Board precedent;

2. The regional director's decision on a substantial factual issue is clearly erroneous on the record and such error prejudicially affects the rights of a party;

3. The conduct of the hearing or any ruling made in connection with the proceeding has resulted in prejudicial error; or

4. There are compelling reasons for reconsideration of an important Board rule or policy.

A request for review should be filed when there is any disagreement with the regional director's decision, since a failure to do so may preclude any further review of the unit issues. The Board's rules provide that:

Failure to request review shall preclude such parties from relitigating, in any related subsequent unfair labor practice proceeding, any issue which was, or could have been, raised in the representation proceeding.

This rule applies when the union wins the election and the employer refuses to bargain on the ground that the regional director's decision was erroneous. The union will then file an unfair labor practice charge, alleging an unlawful refusal to bargain. An employer who failed to request review in the representation case may not then litigate the claimed error in the unfair labor practice case or before a court of appeals.

It should be understood, however, that filing a request for review does not automatically allow an employer to raise these issues in a subsequent unfair labor practice proceeding. If the Board denies the request for review, it will generally deny the employer the opportunity to raise the issues presented in the request for review in a subsequent unfair labor practice proceeding. The employer will, however, have preserved its right to raise the issue before a court of appeals, which eventually may review the Board's decision.

The request for review should take exception to every part of the decision with which there is disagreement. The Board is not required to review every issue decided by the regional director and, even if a request for review is granted, the Board may refuse to consider any issue for which review was not requested.

The regional director ordinarily will schedule the election despite the filing of a request for review. Usually, the Board will act on the request before the election. However, in the event the request for review has not been acted on by the scheduled date for the election, the election will usually be held and the ballots impounded.

In practice, very few requests for review are granted by the Board. When review is granted, the Board will affirm or reverse the decision of the regional director in whole or in part.

EMPLOYEES' NAMES AND ADDRESSES

Within seven days after the regional director's decision directing an election (or within seven days after an election agreement is approved by the regional director), an employer must file with the regional director three copies of a list of the *full* names and addresses of all employees eligible to vote pursuant to the Board's ruling in *Excelsior Underwear Inc.* (1966). The regional director then sends one copy of this list to the union.

When the employer sends the list to the Board, it may desire to write to employees stating, for example:

We did not want to turn over this information, which we have always regarded as confidential. We did so only in response to a written instruction from the NLRB. We regret this invasion of your privacy and any annoyance the union may cause you as a result.

When *Excelsior* was first decided, employers railed at the Board's ruling which prohibited them from visiting the homes of employees, yet required them to provide lists that enabled the union representative to make such visits. The employers' protests, however, fell on deaf ears and a few years later the Supreme Court upheld the rule.

Organizing and the Law, a book written for union organizers, demonstrates how unions use the list as an organizing tool. It states:

Suggestions to Organizers Based on Excelsior

1. Organizing campaigns must include planning geared to the availability of employee address lists after direction of election or employer consent. This planning should consider extensive house calls, phone contacts, and home mailing campaigns in addition to other organizing methods. This should not be a "one-person show" but should be a cooperative effort mobilizing as many key in-house people as possible.

2. All mailings should contain materials designed on a *positive basis.* Unions must realize that they are approaching the worker and the worker's family in their home and

community environment rather than in that of the work-place. They should talk about what the union can accomplish in terms of security for the family breadwinner and economic benefits and protections for the family group. Name calling or attacks upon the employer should be carefully avoided. Mailings should be cleared with organizing directors prior to mailing.

3. These lists must be kept locked in a safe place at all times and never shown or given to any outsider. Misuse of such lists could jeopardize the communications gain made in the *Excelsior* decision.

4. The lists should be tested as soon as possible by mailing campaign literature and checking how many envelopes are returned. The employer may correct these errors, or the information may be used to establish a postelection objection to the accuracy of the list.

5. When an election is won, the list should be preserved. It can come in handy later.

6. If an election is lost, again the mailing list should be preserved. It may be invaluable for a later campaign.

Remember, the techniques made possible by the availability of the mailing lists are not a substitute for a regular campaign or traditional methods but, rather, an aid and adjunct to them.

Getting the list. Organizers should *not* rely on the NLRB automatically making the list available, even though it will do so. Tell the NLRB regional director or an agent that you want the list *as soon as it is received* from the employer. If you are located near the NLRB office, it would be wise to pick up the list. The sooner you have it, the better you can use it to inform those in the unit.[1]

ELECTION ARRANGEMENTS

It is difficult to predict the exact date on which the regional director will issue a decision and direction of election. The complexity of the issues in the particular case has a bearing on the time needed to decide it. Also, circumstances and caseloads vary from region to region. Currently, most regional directors are issuing decisions within forty days from the filing of the petition.

Soon after the issuance of the regional director's decision, the Board agent will request a meeting between the parties to discuss the arrangements for the election. If the parties are geographically wide-

---

[1] Reprinted with permission from the Fourth Edition of *Organizing and The Law*, by Stephen I. Schlossberg and Judith A. Scott. Copyright © 1991 by The Bureau of National Affairs, Inc., Washington, DC 20037.

spread, the arrangements may be made by telephone. The election will be conducted twenty-five to thirty days after the issuance of the regional director's decision and direction of election.

The location for balloting will also be discussed. Elections usually are held on the employer's premises, since it saves the Board rental charges and is convenient for the electorate. However, the balloting place must not be in or near executive or supervisory offices. An area frequented by the employees and away from general supervisory view is appropriate.

On occasion, unions object to holding the election on the employer's premises. The regional director, exercising his or her discretion, may then make arrangements for the balloting to be held elsewhere.

ELIGIBILITY TO VOTE

To be eligible to vote in a Labor Board election, an employee must satisfy two criteria. First, the employee must be employed in the bargaining unit during the payroll period immediately before the regional director approves an election agreement or issues a decision and direction of election. Second, the employee also must be employed on the date of the election.

Employees who have been offered employment but who have not started working during the applicable payroll period are not eligible to vote. Employees on leave and on layoff are eligible to vote as long as they have a reasonable expectation of returning to work. Generally, there are no absentee ballots. An eligible employee must appear at the polls in order to vote, unless the election is held by mail ballot. Employees in the armed forces also are eligible to vote.

MAIL BALLOT ELECTIONS

The Board's Casehandling Manual provides regional directors with discretion to conduct a mail ballot election. While most elections are conducted manually, the guidelines permit the regional director to hold an election by mail "where eligible voters are scattered because of their duties." The Clinton Board has been conducting twice as many mail ballot elections as previous Boards.

About 90% or more of the voters cast ballots in a conventional manual ballot election; generally, no more than about 70% of the eligible voters cast ballots in a mail ballot election. See, for example, *Kwik Care Ltd. v. NLRB* (D.C. Cir. 1996) (66% of the eligible employees cast valid mail ballots) and *Shepard Convention Servs., Inc. v. NLRB* (D.C. Cir. 1996) (17.5% of the eligible employees cast valid mail ballots). Lower participation reduces the number of votes necessary for a union victory, since the election outcome is determined by a majority of those voting and not by a majority of those eligible to vote. Accordingly, in recent years unions have been pressing regional directors to hold mail ballot elections to gain an advantage.

Conversely, employers usually oppose mail ballot elections since, in general, greater voter participation increases the "vote no" count. In addition, employers in mail ballot elections have a realistic concern that union organizers will be able to exert pressure on employees as they mark the ballots in their homes. Also, because of the time necessary to complete the mail ballot process, employers may not conduct group meetings with employees and therefore have fewer opportunities to respond to misstatements by organizers regarding the issues in the election. (See discussion of 24-hour rule below). However, where a mail ballot is unavoidable, to counter the possibility of a low voter turnout, the employer should make a special effort to get out the vote after the ballots have been mailed.

The procedure for conducting a mail ballot election is prescribed in the Board's Casehandling Manual at section 11336. Briefly, the regional office sends each eligible voter an election kit. It contains "Instructions to Eligible Employees Voting by United States Mail" (**Illustration No. 30** at page 160), a ballot (**Illustration No. 31** at page 161), a blue envelope in which to insert the ballot (**Illustration No. 32** at page 162), and a pre-addressed yellow envelope in which the blue envelope is placed (**Illustration No. 33** at page 163). An "identification stub" is contained on the back of the yellow envelope.

The instructions state the date by which the ballot must be returned to the regional office. The date selected depends upon the circumstances, as agreed upon by the parties during the preelection arrangements. Ballots may not be sent to employees on layoff, unless all parties agree. The ballot count follows the same procedure as in a manual election (see Chapter XVIII), with one difference. Because the ballots already have been marked, the employer may designate a supervisory employee as an observer and the labor organization may designate a union official to observe the opening and counting of the ballots.

Application of 24-Hour Rule

The Board's rule prohibiting "captive audience" meetings within 24 hours of the opening of the election polls (see Chapter XVII at page 197) also applies to mail ballot elections:

Employers and unions alike will be prohibited from making election speeches on company time to massed assemblies of employees within the period set forth in the notice, i.e., from the time and date on which the "mail in" ballots are scheduled to be dispatched by the Regional Office until the terminal time and date prescribed for their return. Violations of this rule by employers or unions will cause an election to be set aside whenever valid objections are filed. *Oregon Wash. Tel. Co.* (1959).

The Board continues to apply this rule. The effect of the rule is a prohibition against such speeches over a longer period of time. In *American Red Cross Blood Servs.* (1996), for example, the Regional Director mailed ballots to the employees on March 1, 1996. Three days later, the employer conducted two "captive audience" meetings. Notwithstanding a majority vote against the union, the Board ordered a new election.

* * *

The filing and processing of a representation petition is preliminary to the major event—the election campaign and balloting. These important matters are discussed in the following chapters.

ILLUSTRATION NO. 29

UNITED STATES OF AMERICA
NATIONAL LABOR RELATIONS BOARD
STIPULATED ELECTION AGREEMENT

The parties agree that a hearing is waived, that approval of this Agreement constitutes withdrawal of any notice of hearing previously issued in this matter, that the petition is amended to conform to this Agreement, and further **AGREE AS FOLLOWS:**

1.   **SECRET BALLOT.** A secret-ballot election shall be held under the supervision of the Regional Director in the unit defined below at the agreed time and place, under the Board's Rules and Regulations.

2.   **ELIGIBLE VOTERS.** The eligible voters shall be unit employees employed during the payroll period for eligibility, including employees who did not work during that period because they were ill, on vacation, or temporarily laid off, employees engaged in an economic strike which commenced less than 12 months before the election date and who retained their status as such during the eligibility period and their replacements, and employees in the military services of the United States who appear in person at the polls. Ineligible to vote are employees who have quit or been discharged for cause since the payroll period for eligibility, employees engaged in a strike who have been discharged for cause since the commencement thereof and who have not been rehired or reinstated before the election date, and employees engaged in an economic strike which commenced more than 12 months before the election date and who have been permanently replaced. The employer shall provide to the Regional Director, within 7 days after the Regional Director has approved this Agreement, an election eligibility list containing the names and addresses of all eligible voters. **Excelsior Underwear, Inc.,** 156 NLRB 1236.

3.   **NOTICE OF ELECTION.** Copies of the Notice of Election shall be posted by the Employer in conspicuous places and usual posting places easily accessible to the voters at least three (3) full working days prior to 12:01 a.m. of the day of the election. As soon as the election arrangements are finalized, the Employer will be informed when the Notices must be posted in order to comply with the posting requirement. Failure to post the Election Notices as required shall be grounds for setting aside the election whenever proper and timely objections are filed.

4.   **ACCOMMODATIONS REQUIRED.** All parties should notify the Regional Director as soon as possible of any voters, potential voters, or other participants in this election who have handicaps falling within the provisions of Section 504 of the Rehabilitation Act of 1973, as amended, and 29 C.F.R. 100.603, and who in order to participate in this election need appropriate auxiliary aids, as defined in 29 C.F.R. 100.603, and request the necessary assistance.

5.   **OBSERVERS.** Each party may station an equal number of authorized, nonsupervisory-employee observers at the polling places to assist in the election, to challenge the eligibility of voters, and to verify the tally.

6.   **TALLY OF BALLOTS.** Upon conclusion of the election, the ballots will be counted and a tally of ballots prepared and immediately made available to the parties.

7.   **POSTELECTION AND RUNOFF PROCEDURES.** All procedures after the ballots are counted shall conform with the Board's Rules and Regulations.

8.   **RECORD.** The record in this case shall include this Agreement and be governed by the Board's Rules and Regulations.

9. COMMERCE. The Employer is engaged in commerce within the meaning of Section 2(6) and (7) of the National Labor Relations Act and a question affecting commerce has arisen concerning the representation of employees within the meaning of Section 9(c). *(Insert commerce facts.)*

10. WORDING ON THE BALLOT. When only one labor organization is on the ballot, the choice shall be "Yes" or "No". If more than one labor organization is on the ballot, the choices shall appear as follows, reading left to right or top to bottom. *(If more than one labor organization is on the ballot, any labor organization may have its name removed by the approval of the Regional Director of a timely written request.)*

First.

Second.

Third.

11. PAYROLL PERIOD FOR ELIGIBILITY - THE PERIOD ENDING _____

12. DATE, HOURS, AND PLACE OF ELECTION.

13. THE APPROPRIATE COLLECTIVE-BARGAINING UNIT.

(Employer)	_(Labor Organization)_
By _____ _____	By _____ _____
(Name) _(Date)_	_(Name)_ _(Date)_
_____	_____
(Title)	_(Title)_

Recommended:

_____ _____
(Board Agent) _(Date)_

Date approved _____

_____
(Labor Organization)

By _____

(Name) _(Date)_

Regional Director
National Labor Relations Board

_____
(Title)

Case _____

ILLUSTRATION NO. 30

FORM NLRB-4175
(12/94)

United States of America
National Labor Relations Board

Instructions to Eligible Employees Voting By
United States Mail

INSTRUCTIONS

1. MARK YOUR BALLOT IN SECRET BY PLACING AN X IN THE APPROPRIATE BOX. MAKE NO OTHER MARKS ON YOUR BALLOT.

2. IT IS IMPORTANT TO MAINTAIN THE SECRECY OF YOUR BALLOT. DO NOT SHOW YOUR BALLOT TO ANYONE AFTER YOU HAVE MARKED IT.

3. PUT YOUR BALLOT IN THE BLUE ENVELOPE AND SEAL THE ENVELOPE.

4. PUT BLUE ENVELOPE CONTAINING THE BALLOT INTO THE YELLOW ADDRESSED RETURN ENVELOPE.

5. SIGN THE BACK OF THE YELLOW RETURN ENVELOPE ON THE SPACE PROVIDED.

6. MAIL IMMEDIATELY. NO POSTAGE IS REQUIRED.

For further information, call the Regional Office at **(215) 597-7646**
National Labor Relations Board, Region Four
615 Chestnut Street, Seventh Floor
Philadelphia, PA 19106-4404

TO BE COUNTED, YOUR BALLOT MUST REACH THE REGIONAL OFFICE
BY: **Monday, June 24, 1996.**

ILLUSTRATION NO. 31

UNITED STATES OF AMERICA
ESTADOS UNIDOS DE AMERICA

National Labor Relations Board
Junta Nacional De Relaciones Del Trabajo

OFFICIAL SECRET BALLOT
PAPELETA SECRETA OFICIAL
For Certain Employees of
Para Ciertos Empleados De

Do you wish to be represented for purposes of collective bargaining by—
¿Desea usted estar representado para los fines de negociar colectivamente por

HIGHWAY AND LOCAL MOTOR FREIGHT DRIVERS' LOCAL UNION 707,
INTERNATIONAL BROTHERHOOD OF TEAMSTERS, AFL-CIO?

MARK AN "X" IN THE SQUARE OF YOUR CHOICE
MARQUESE CON UNA "X" DENTRO DEL CUADRO DE SU SELECCION

YES SI	NO NO

DO NOT SIGN THIS BALLOT. Fold and drop in ballot box.
NO FIRME ESTA PAPELETA. Dóblela y depósitela en la urna electoral.

If you spoil this ballot return it to the Board Agent for a new one.
Si usted daña esta papeleta devuélvala al Agente de la Junta y pídale una nueva.

ILLUSTRATION NO. 32

BLUE ENVELOPE

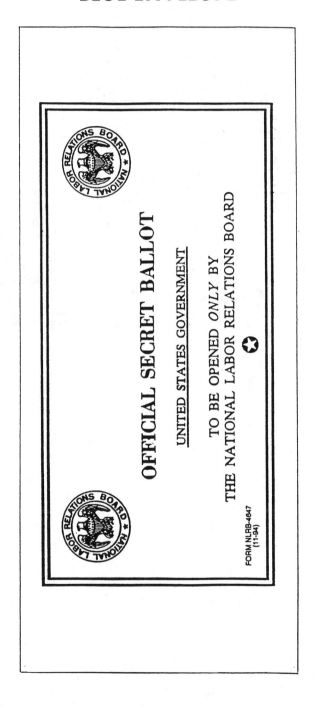

ILLUSTRATION NO. 33

YELLOW ENVELOPE

UNITED STATES GOVERNMENT
NATIONAL LABOR RELATIONS BOARD
REGION 4
615 CHESTNUT STREET - 7TH FLOOR
PHILADELPHIA, PA 19106-4404
An Equal Opportunity Employer

OFFICIAL BUSINESS
Penalty for Private Use, $300.

NATIONAL LABOR RELATIONS BOARD
REGION 4
615 CHESTNUT STREET - 7TH FLOOR
PHILADELPHIA, PA 19106-4404

IDENTIFICATION STUB

Sign Your Name Here. Be Sure To Sign DO NOT Print.

I BELIEVE I AM AN ELIGIBLE VOTER.
I PERSONALLY VOTED THE WITHIN BALLOT.

CASE NUMBER

ELIGIBILITY KEY NUMBER

BACK OF ENVELOPE

CHAPTER XVI

AN ILLUSTRATIVE MANAGEMENT COUNTER-CAMPAIGN

(THE FIRST THREE WEEKS)

Voters in political campaigns generally vote against a candidate rather than for one. The same is true in a union election. The employer should give voters a variety of reasons and arguments for voting *against* the union, by emphasizing the costs, risks, and obligations which employees would face with union representation.

Generally, a union's highest level of employee support is on the day it files the petition. While the law requires signatures from only 30% of the unit employees, most unions wait until they have accumulated more than 50%. When the union files its petition, there may be a core of employees who solidly support the union, often as many as 25%. There also may be a core of solid management support, again 25%. The remaining employees are "on the fence" and will be the primary target of the employer's and union's preelection effort.

Where the parties have entered into a stipulated election agreement, the agreement will include the date of the election. Where, instead, a hearing has been held, the election will be held 25 to 30 calendar days after the regional director issues the decision and direction of election.

While the parties wait for the regional director's decision and direction of election, the union's campaign and management's counter-campaign are low key with a minimum of literature and muted polemics. There is an important reason for this hiatus: the campaigns must reach their peak on election day. If the campaign is too long, employees will lose interest.

As soon as the election date is fixed, the employer should prepare a calendar of activities, along with proposed communications. The calendar should be viewed as a tentative plan to be modified and supplemented as the campaign progresses. The preelection calendar in **Illustration No. 34** at page 167, schedules activities for each of the 19 workdays immediately preceding the election.

Once the regional director directs the election or the election date is agreed upon in a stipulated election agreement the campaigns escalate. Each party uses its most effective and persuasive techniques and arguments building toward peak support on election day. The union's efforts focus on home visits (its most effective technique), large group meetings, and written communications aimed at the employer's most vulnerable areas. The employer shifts its attention from the agency proceedings to communications that will force the union into a defensive posture and convince the employees to reject the union.

This chapter and the next one illustrate a typical, four-week management campaign. Each day's activities are commented on. Illustrations of supporting materials are provided at the end of the chapters. Although these materials have been effective in actual campaigns, a "canned" approach is not recommended. Every workforce presents a different set of circumstances. Campaign materials should be tailored to the particular issues or situation.

ILLUSTRATION NO. 34

PREELECTION CALENDAR

Week	Monday	Tuesday	Wednesday	Thursday	Friday
1	*Day 1* *Receive* NLRB Decision *Meet* with supervisors *Post* election arrangements	*Day 2* *Presentation:* All employees, large group *Handout* by supervisors	*Day 3* *Mail* letter to homes	*Day 4* *Handout* by supervisors	*Day 5* *Submit:* Voter eligibility list to NLRB
2	*Day 6* *Meet* with supervisors *Poster*	*Day 7* *Handout* by supervisors *Mail* letter to homes	*Day 8* *Presentation:* All employees, small groups	*Day 9* *Handout* by supervisors	*Day 10* *(Payday)* *Paycheck Stuffer*
3	*Day 11* *Meet* with supervisors *Handout* by supervisors: Contest	*Day 12* *Poster* *Mail* letter to homes	*Day 13* *Presentation:* All employees, small groups *Handout* by supervisors	*Day 14* *Poster*	*Day 15* *Handout* by supervisors
4	*Day 16* *Post:* Official Notice of Election *Meet* with supervisors	*Day 17* *Mail* letter to homes *Handout* by supervisors	*Day 18* *Meet* with supervisors *Announce:* Contest winner on bulletin board	*Day 19* *Presentation:* All employees, large group *Handout* by supervisors	*Day 20* *(Payday)* ELECTION DAY

COMMENTARY ON PREELECTION CALENDAR

DAY 1

After receiving the regional director's decision and direction of election (or after a stipulated election agreement is entered into), the employer should hold a meeting with all supervisors and specify which employees are eligible (and ineligible) to vote. During the next four weeks, the employer should hold frequent meetings with its supervisors.

Bulletin Board Posting

All employer communications about the union campaign should be posted on a special bulletin board. The election arrangements should be posted as soon as they become available. The sample notice illustrated at page 173 includes the election date and times for voting as well as an explanation of who is eligible to vote. Strategically, it is desirable to have this information come first from the employer rather than the union.

DAY 2

Group Presentation

The employer's initial presentation should set the tone for its campaign. The talk outlined at pages 174 and 175 advises employees what they can expect to see and hear from both parties and emphasizes the importance of considering all the facts before voting.

Supervisory Handout

A handout from the supervisor is an effective way to underscore the employer's message, while providing an opportunity to discuss employee reactions to it. The handout also may help the supervisor discern problems, concerns, or interests to be addressed in subsequent communications. The supervisory handout reproduced at page 176 suggests questions for employees to ask the union representative about the hidden costs and risks of unionization.

DAY 3

Home Mailing

Home mailings bring the significance of the union election to the family. An employee may be influenced by a family member who is unaware, but appropriately concerned, about the consequences of unionization. The sample letter illustrated at page 177 discusses matters the union *cannot* impose on the company, but *can* impose on employees.

DAY 4

Supervisory Handout

The supervisory handout appearing at page 178 addresses common misperceptions about the labor movement. Graphics help to illustrate the steady decline in overall unionization among American workers.

DAY 5

Voter Eligibility List

The *Excelsior* list of eligible voters discussed in the previous chapter must be submitted to the regional director within seven days after the regional director issues the decision directing an election (or within seven days after a stipulated election agreement is approved). Failure to do so will be grounds for overturning the election results.

DAY 6

Poster

Even if employees have signed authorization cards, they may change their minds and vote against the union. The illustrative poster at page 179 reinforces the message that employees have the right to change their minds.

DAY 7

Supervisory Handout

The union is a business which organizes employees in order to generate revenues. Like all businesses, its survival depends upon income from "customers"—in this case, employee members who pay for its services. It uses the income generated from dues to pay union expenses, including the salaries of union officials. The supervisory handout, "Where does your money go?" (illustrated at page 180), makes this point and gives the supervisor an opportunity to show the employee a copy of the union's financial statement on file with the Department of Labor (See Chapter X at pages 85 and 86).

Home Mailing

Unions have the power to fine members for certain offenses. The risk of a fine should be communicated to employees. Union fines are documented in official decisions of the Labor Board and occasionally cited in newspaper articles. The amount can be substantial, depending on the nature of the offense. Providing employees with examples of fines from actual Board cases can be persuasive as demonstrated at page 181. A newspaper report of union fines is particularly effective where it involves the same union or is from the same geographical area as shown at page 182.

DAY 8

Small Group Presentation

Speaking to a small group of employees permits an intimate setting and provides an effective forum for discussing the issues and the arguments dominating the campaign. The presentation outlined at pages 183 and 184 focuses on the company's growth and how the union could have a negative impact on its future.

DAY 9

Supervisory Handout

The handout in the form of a questionnaire, illustrated at pages 185 and 186, is an effective way of providing employees with information. Of course, it requires follow-up by supervisors who have the correct answers.

Day 10

Split Paycheck Stuffer

Some employers dramatize the costs of union membership by deducting the amount of monthly dues from the paycheck and giving it to the employee in a separate envelope. The envelope may say on the outside: "This envelope contains $20 of your money, the minimum amount the union would take out of a member's paycheck every month."

The use of the split paycheck is permitted by the Labor Board, except within the 24 hours immediately preceding the election and during the polling. The Board similarly restricts changes in the time, location, and method of paycheck distribution during this period. *Kalin Constr. Co., Inc.* (1996).

DAY 11

Supervisory Handout

Employers sometimes sponsor contests to generate employee interest and involvement in the campaign. In the handout reproduced at page 187, employees are asked questions which direct their attention to the issues of fines and strikes: "What is the largest fine ever levied against a member of this union?"; "What was the length of the union's longest strike?" Entries must be numbered so that participating employees do not disclose their identities. Employees keep entry form receipts and the winning number is announced shortly before the election. (See Day 18 Preelection Calendar).

The Labor Board has held that contests offering modest cash or merchandise prizes are lawful as long as the prize is not contingent upon voting or the outcome of the election. For example, in *Sony Corp. of Am.* (1993), the Board held that a television set valued at $167 was not of such substantial value to warrant setting aside a decertification election.

DAY 12

Poster

Promises of better economic or working conditions often are used by unions to persuade employees to vote "yes." They are deemed campaign puffery by the Labor Board and are lawful. A poster challenging the union to *guarantee* these promises (and others they may have made) in writing, as illustrated at page 188, is an effective reminder that the promises are often empty.

Home Mailing

An employer is free to hire permanent replacements for *economic* strikers and may refuse a permanently replaced striker's request for reinstatement. However, strikers who unconditionally apply for reinstatement are entitled to be reinstated if no replacements have been hired for their positions at the time they apply or when their replacements vacate these positions, unless the strikers have acquired regular and substantially equivalent employment elsewhere. Employer statements about the risk of permanent replacement must not imply otherwise.

The letter reproduced at page 189, which discusses the risks of strikes and the law of striker replacement in non-technical terms, can be persuasive to the employee and the employee's family.

DAY 13

Small Group Presentation

The union's strongest argument is the promise of better terms and conditions of employment through contract negotiations. However, the law clearly states that neither party is required to agree to any proposal or make any concession. Precise information on how the collective bargaining process *really* works is one of the most important messages of a management campaign. The small-group presentation outlined at pages 190 and 191 is an effective format for conveying this information.

Supervisory Handout

The message about the uncertainty of negotiations discussed in the small-group meeting should be reinforced with a supervisory handout. The handout, "The Truth about Negotiations," reproduced at page 192, illustrates the major points.

DAY 14

Poster

When the parties cannot reach an agreement at the bargaining table, the union may call a strike to pressure the employer to make concessions. The risk of a strike is one of the most important arguments against union representation. The poster shown at page 193 effectively depicts this reality.

DAY 15

Supervisory Handout

The personal "strike-cost calculator" at page 194 demonstrates with hard numbers how long it would take employees to recover financially from a strike. The hourly rates in the illustration should reflect the actual wages.

* * *

The final week of the campaign is discussed in the next chapter.

DAY 1

BULLETIN BOARD POSTING

LABOR BOARD ELECTION

We have set the time and date for the Labor Board election. We arranged it so that all eligible employees can vote at convenient times when they are at work. Here are the details:

DATE: JANUARY 29

TIME: 8 A.M. TO 9 A.M. AND

                 3 P.M. TO 4 P.M.

PLACE: STOCK ROOM

WHO IS ELIGIBLE TO VOTE?

All regular full-time and part-time production and maintenance employees, including group leaders, warehouse employees, and shipping and receiving clerks.

Regardless of whether you signed a card for the union, your secret ballot vote should reflect your *current* thinking.

Think for yourself—**VOTE "NO."**

DAY 2

GROUP PRESENTATION TO ALL EMPLOYEES

I. INTRODUCTION

I would like to take a few moments today to discuss a decision you will be making later this month which could last a lifetime—to vote for or against the union.

A. Importance of Voting

> It is very important that *all* eligible voters actually participate **and vote**, whether or not you signed a card. Not voting helps the union, since the union needs a simple majority of the votes actually cast to win.

> You can't "stay out of it" now. This is your plant and your job which will be affected even if you don't vote.

B. Responsibilities

1. Your Responsibility: Listen to both sides. Understand the huge differences between wishful thinking and reality. Ask as many questions as you have. Feel free to speak up and voice your opinion.

2. Our Responsibility: To give you all the facts so that you can make the right decision on election day.

C. How We Will Communicate

1. By written communication (letters, bulletin board postings, and handouts). Please pay careful attention to all the information.

2. By direct personal contact (always backed up with documented facts) from your supervisor and others in management.

II. WHAT TO EXPECT FROM THE UNION

- The union will make a sales pitch. Based on the way this union has acted and operated in the past we have a pretty good idea what they will try to do.

- They will call the company "liars" and the information we provide misleading. They won't admit that the company has absolutely nothing to gain from giving you wrong information.

- They will tell you that negotiations are quick, simple, and easy—and that you should expect to receive the same kinds of policies and benefits in effect elsewhere. They won't admit that our company is a world apart from other companies and what those companies may be able to provide has got nothing to do with us.

● They will tell you that you have "nothing to lose" by giving the union a chance to negotiate for you. They won't tell you that every single wage provision and benefit term that now exists is subject to change and could be reduced as a result of negotiations.

● They will tell you that you need not worry about a strike, because a strike would be "impossible" at this company. They won't tell you about our commitments to our customers and that we would have to operate during a strike.

● They will say you do not stand any risk at all in voting the union in because you do not need to join or become a dues-paying member. But they won't tell you about the pressure to join from the union and fellow employees, nor will they tell you that their first bargaining proposal will be a requirement that every employee join the union and pay dues.

III. CONCLUSION

In conclusion, please remember the following:

Listen carefully to all they have to say, then insist that the union give you proof and guarantees—do not settle for promises. Ask questions. Demand straight answers.

As we get closer to election day, I would like you to think about your decision in terms of what is best for you. Listen to all of the facts, consider the risks, determine the odds, and vote for what you think is your best chance at coming out ahead. There is no doubt in my mind you won't put your future in the hands of this union. Thank you.

DAY 2

SUPERVISORY HANDOUT

STOP! THINK! ASK QUESTIONS! LISTEN!

Organizers from the union are trained salespeople. The product they try to sell is union representation. It isn't free. If you speak with one of them, ask for answers to the following questions before you make a decision.

Isn't it true that:

* It will cost me dues each and every month to be a member of the union?

* If a member violates a union rule, he or she can be fined by the union, and that there's no limit on how high that fine could be?

* Nothing is guaranteed to change or improve just because a union is in the picture?

* I could be called out on strike?

* Economic strikers get no wages or benefits as an employee while striking?

* Economic strikers can be replaced—permanently—while on strike and may not have a job to come back to if all positions have been filled?

UNLESS YOU GET STRAIGHT, HONEST ANSWERS, YOU ARE BETTER OFF NOT TAKING ANY CHANCES.

DAY 3

HOME MAILING

Dear Fellow Employee:

The union organizers have distributed a leaflet claiming the union will be able to deliver on all its promises. You should know the law allows the union to make promises to you, even though the law does *not* require the union to deliver. *Remember,* it is your company which pays your wages and provides you with your benefits. No one—including a union—can force us to do anything which does not make good business sense.

We want you to understand the difference between fact and fiction.

First, let us look at what the union *cannot* force your company to do:

1. THE UNION *CANNOT* force the company to agree to any request the company is unwilling or unable to accept.

2. THE UNION *CANNOT* force the company to increase any wages or benefits unless the company believes it is in its best interest to do so.

3. THE UNION *CANNOT* guarantee job security or furnish you regular work.

Now let us take a look at what the union *can* force employees to do:

1. THE UNION *CAN* force employees to pay dues each and every month when there is a union security clause in the contract.

2. THE UNION *CAN* force members to stand trial and pay fines for violation of any of the provisions of its "book of rules" (Constitution).

3. THE UNION *CAN* force members to pay extra assessments whenever the union treasury requires more money.

Consider the many advantages and benefits you now enjoy without a union. When you do so, I am sure you will vote "NO."

Sincerely,

DAY 4

SUPERVISORY HANDOUT

ASK FOR FACTS

There are some very important questions you should ask those who are pushing the union. If having a union is such a great deal, then...

(1) Why has this union lost 115,000 members in the past ten years?

(2) Why have unions lost almost 4 million members since 1978?

(3) Why are more than 4 out of 5 employees in private industry not represented by a union?

(4) Why have employees in 5,000 companies thrown their unions out in the past ten years?

(5) Why have hundreds of thousands of union members lost their jobs because of layoffs and plant closings?

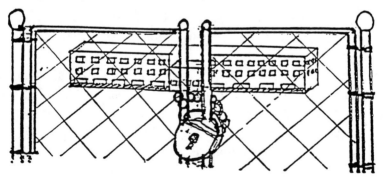

DAY 6

POSTER

ONLY YOUR VOTE COUNTS

What if you signed a card???

The card is *not* important now. *You can still vote* NO!

Sometimes, employees who really do not want a union sign union cards. They may have been pressured; they may have been misled; or they may have misunderstood the significance of signing.

The *Law* protects you:

YOU *CAN* CHANGE YOUR MIND.

YOU *CAN* VOTE AGAINST THE UNION, EVEN IF YOU SIGNED UP OR WENT TO UNION MEETINGS.

REMEMBER... If the union somehow wins, it will make decisions for *everyone* eligible to vote. **VOTE NO.**

DAY 7

SUPERVISORY HANDOUT

Where does your money go?

Look at the Electrical Workers' most recent LM-2 (financial statement). Your supervisor can show you a copy. They spent money on everything except the dues-paying members.

DAY 7

HOME MAILING

Dear Fellow Employee:

I wrote to you on Wednesday about union fines. They are used by unions to punish members for violating union-made rules. The following are actual cases in which union members have been fined by their unions:

Reasons	*Amount of Fines*
A union member attended church instead of a union meeting	$ 5.00
A union member exceeded union-set production quotas	$ 100.00
A union member refused to comply with the order of a union business agent	$ 300.00
A union member filed unfair labor practice charges against the union	$ 450.00
A union member informed the company that a fellow union member violated a company rule	$ 500.00
A union member made derogatory remarks about the union and its officials	$1,000.00
A union member refused to join a strike	$2,000.00
Union members returned to work during a strike	$2,500.00

Union fines are legal debts, collectible in court. The attached article shows what happened to 13 union members when they crossed picket lines to return to work. Avoid the risks. VOTE NO!

Sincerely,

DAY 7

HOME MAILING

13 Butchers Sue Detroit Union

DETROIT - Thirteen members of United Food and Commercial Workers Local 539 (meatcutters) are suing their union, claiming it violated an amnesty agreement made as part of a strike settlement last year.

The nine-day strike, involving 629 members of the local who work for Borman's, was called to protest a $.92-an-hour wage cut and scaled back benefits imposed by the company.

The suit claims the strike settlement called for amnesty for all parties involved. However, the members charge, the local violated the terms of the amnesty by publishing the names of those who had crossed picket lines and by fining them.

Dick Phillips, president of Local 539, admitted the workers had been fined and their names published in the local's publication. But he also said there was no amnesty agreement.

Phillips said the board had "tried" 14 workers who crossed picket lines. Thirteen were found guilty and one was acquitted. The 13 were fined $2,500 each.

He said several of those fined had appealed the action to the international union. Those who had filed "timely" appeals succeeded in getting their fines reduced, but he did not have the exact figures.

Phillips said that if the fines aren't paid, the meatcutters could be suspended. He said the lawsuit apparently is an attempt to stop such suspensions.

In the meantime, he said the union has filed suit against two of the 13 meatcutters to get them to pay their fines. Phillips said the suits had been filed before the present joint suit by the members. The union plans to file two suits at a time and eventually sue all 13 members, Phillips added.

DAY 8

SMALL-GROUP PRESENTATION

I. INTRODUCTION

Today, I would like to review with you what we have done to improve our work lives and make our future secure here by working together *without* outsiders. I will also explain how having a union here could affect us.

II. UNION-FREE; FLEXIBILITY AND GROWTH

Let us review how we, as a union-free workplace, have been able to provide stable jobs with good pay and benefits over the years. We are proud of our track record and hope you share that pride.

1. We have installed new equipment.

2. Employee training has been stepped up to provide people with the necessary skills to do their jobs properly.

3. Wage and benefit adjustments have been made on a regular basis, providing you with a very competitive package.

These improvements were made for two reasons:

1. To provide you a better, more fulfilling work life; and

2. To maintain the quality of our product and the efficiency with which it is produced so we can meet the needs of our customers.

III. HOW A UNION COULD AFFECT OUR FUTURE

We chose this location from among many towns which wanted to have our investments and the jobs we would provide. One of the objectives we established was to operate on a *union-free* basis. Being *union-free* is important to our business, especially given the intense competition we face every day in the marketplace.

Why? One reason is that our *customers* appreciate the fact that we are union-free. They know that, without a union, there will be no risk of a strike to interrupt or delay delivery of their orders.

Second, we are more capable of delivering a *quality* product, on time. Being union-free means we are free of the illogical and impractical work restrictions which a union often causes.

Third, our quality is a direct result of our ability to work as a team and not as adversaries—that can all change if a union comes in. I know. I have worked at unionized plants before. I have seen firsthand how a union creates an "us versus them" atmosphere. The union could try to build walls between us and fabricate issues to position itself to "look good."

I believe most of you do not want to work as adversaries and our customers certainly do not want that to happen. They know how unions often affect productivity. And if our productivity is hurt by a strike or work restrictions, we risk losing our customers.

IV. CONCLUSION

We are all looking for long-term job security. We strongly believe our union-free status gives us the best chance for success.

Thanks for your attention.

DAY 9

SUPERVISORY HANDOUT

DO YOU KNOW THE ANSWERS
TO THESE QUESTIONS?

1. (A) The *average* wage increase for *union* members last year was:

    a.   0%

    b.   2%

    c.   3%

    d.   4%

    (B) The *average* wage increase for *our* employees last year was:

    a.   0%

    b.   2%

    c.   3%

    d.   4%

    e.   over 4%

2. What economic improvements have our employees received in the last year?

    a.   Trainer's bonus

    b.   Insurance refund plan

    c.   Healthy baby benefit

    d.   Two wage increases

    e.   All of the above

3. Which of the following benefits that you now have could be *reduced* as a result of union negotiations?

    a. Company paid holidays

    b. Company paid vacations

    c. Shift differential

    d. Insurance coverage

    e. All of the above

4. Which of the following are *guaranteed* to improve if the union wins the election?

    a. Wages

    b. Benefits

    c. Working conditions

    d. None of the above

5. During the entire time a contract is being negotiated, the company is prohibited from making special improvements in wages or benefits on its own.

    __True   __False

DAY 11

SUPERVISORY HANDOUT

"WIN A TV SET"

All you have to do is guess the amount of the largest *fine* ever imposed on a member of the union and the length of the *longest strike* called by the union.

The union says it does not fine members. It also denies its reputation for strikes. But we all know differently. What you may not know is just how big the fines can be and how long strikes can last.

To enter the contest, tear off the entry blank below and write in your answer. The winner will be the entry coming closest to the correct answers in both categories. In case of a tie, there will be a drawing for the winner.

Each person may enter once. Boxes for your entry will be in the cafeteria and near the time clock.

A portable TV set is the winning prize. Be sure to keep your numbered receipt. Do not sign your name. The contest will close one week from today.

Receipt No. 1

I believe the largest fine ever levied against a member of this union was $____

I believe the longest strike has lasted __ days, __ months, or __ years.

DAY 12

POSTER

WILL THE UNION PUT ITS MONEY WHERE ITS MOUTH IS?

Ask the union salesperson if the union will *guarantee*—not just promise—that the union will *deliver* everything promised.

Ask for a *signed, notarized, legally enforceable* GUARANTEE (use that word) about *any* of the following:

1. I *guarantee* you will get an *immediate* pay raise of _____ (fill in what you've been promised) per hour in our first contract.

2. I *guarantee* you will not *lose* any of your current wages or benefits as long as you are represented by my union.

3. I *guarantee* if you are called out on an economic strike, your job will not be filled by a *permanent replacement*.

The union won't guarantee these promises, because it can't. **TALK IS CHEAP. VOTE NO.**

Day 12

HOME MAILING

Dear Fellow Employee:

The union election is next week. Before you vote we especially ask you to consider the possibility of a strike.

A strike affects everyone. But, the effects of a strike are hardest on you and your family. Most of you have never been through a strike. You're lucky, because a strike can be an ugly and frightening experience. During strikes, employees have been threatened and assaulted, and their cars damaged.

Why do unions call strikes? There are many reasons. Many times prior to an election such as this one, the union makes a lot of promises to employees to persuade them to vote for the union. During negotiations, however, the Company has the right to say *no* to the union's demands. The union has only three choices: (1) keep bargaining to try to convince the Company to change; (2) give up; or (3) try to force a change in the Company's position by calling a strike.

What happens during a strike and what does it mean to you? To begin with, *you don't get paid if you go on strike.* The Company has *the right to stop paying premiums for your health insurance coverage* while you are not working. If that happened, you would have to arrange to pay the entire premium. During a strike, *your bills do not stop.* You still have to make rent or mortgage payments. Your car payments are still due and you still have to pay for food. The fact is, employees and their families are the ones who get "stuck" during a strike.

The Company has the right to continue operating if employees go out on strike. We can do this by hiring permanent replacements to fill the jobs of those employees who go out on an economic strike. When the strike is over, the permanent replacements have the right to keep their jobs and the strikers only have a right to come back *if a position is available.* If there are no openings, the strikers must wait until a position becomes available. Strikers are put on a preferential recall list for future job openings. Sometimes strikers have to wait six months or longer before a position becomes available.

I am not saying that there is definitely going to be a strike here. However, strikes are always a possibility. If I were in your position, I would not take the risk. Vote *NO* on election day.

Sincerely,

DAY 13

SMALL-GROUP PRESENTATION

I. INTRODUCTION

I'll bet most employees here have never been involved in contract negotiations. So it's not that surprising if a lot of people think having a union negotiate for them is a no-risk, no-lose deal. That may be what the union wants you to believe. Unfortunately, *that is just not true.*

II. THE UNION WOULD REPRESENT EVERY EMPLOYEE ELIGIBLE TO VOTE

Some of you may think that if you didn't sign a card for the union, don't vote for the union, or if you don't join the union, then you are not involved. *That is not the way it works.* The law says that if the union is voted in, it will become the spokesperson for *each and every* employee who was *eligible* to vote! If you are included in the voting unit and the union somehow wins, the union would become *your* spokesperson.

III. NEGOTIATIONS

There is absolutely *nothing* in the law that says a company has to agree to what a union may ask for. The law of negotiations is in the National Labor Relations Act. That law discusses the obligations of an employer and a union at the bargaining table. Here is what that *law* actually says:

> To bargain collectively is . . . to meet at reasonable times and confer in good faith with respect to wages, hours, and other terms and conditions of employment . . . **BUT SUCH OBLIGATION DOES NOT COMPEL EITHER PARTY TO AGREE TO A PROPOSAL OR REQUIRE THE MAKING OF A CONCESSION.**

The *only* thing that the union would get if it won would be the chance to sit down and talk to us. We would bargain in good faith, listen, and discuss everything the union wanted to talk about. *But make no mistake*—if we felt that the union's demands were not in the best interests of the company, for any reason, we would have the lawful right to say *"NO."*

Some people are even being told that once the union is voted in, anything they don't want or don't like is going to change. But that is *not* the case. The union cannot force the company to change a practice which the company feels is necessary to remain competitive. If we did, we wouldn't be in business very long.

Now, let's talk about what the *union* wants most in the contract. Unfortunately for you, it may not be the same thing you may want.

The union will want a "dues checkoff" clause in the contract. This clause is a pretty tough pill for employees to swallow. It requires the company to take out union *dues and initiation fees and assessments automatically* from your paycheck. You wouldn't even have a say as to whether you needed your money for yourself and your family that month. The money would be deducted *before* you even saw your check, month after month after month.

IV. WHAT CAN THE UNION DO IF WE SAY NO?

Consider what could happen if we said *no* in negotiations to something the union wants badly. The union could call a strike. *No one,* including me, is saying that a strike *definitely* would happen here. But with a union, there is *always* that possibility.

A strike would certainly affect our company. If we are not able to meet our customers' delivery requirements due to a strike, the customer has the right to buy from someone else who can deliver without additional costs and delays. And if the strike lasts awhile, we may never be able to get the customer back. Pure and simple—a strike could mean the possible loss of orders. And without orders, there are no jobs.

Strikes are nasty for everyone concerned, not just for the companies involved, but especially for those employees who *have* to work to make ends meet. You may have seen cases where employees crossed picket lines so they could support their families, only to be charged with a violation of union rules and fined the equivalent of a day's wages for *each* day they worked during the strike.

V. CONCLUSION

We hope this helps you better understand the facts about union representation and negotiations. As with everything else we've shared with you since this started, what we have told you today may sound harsh, but it's all true. And I challenge the union to prove otherwise.

Thank you.

DAY 13

SUPERVISORY HANDOUT

THE TRUTH ABOUT NEGOTIATIONS

THERE ARE NO GUARANTEES ONCE NEGOTIATIONS BEGIN:

1. You are *NOT* guaranteed to receive a single improvement (even one cent more) in wages or benefits just because you're a union member.

2. You are *NOT* guaranteed your current benefits after the union concludes negotiations. (You could *lose* something you've got now).

3. You are *NOT* guaranteed you can pay all your bills if negotiations break down and the union calls you out on strike.

4. You are *NOT* guaranteed you won't be permanently replaced during a strike.

FOR *NO* NEGOTIATION RISKS, VOTE NO

DAY 14

POSTER

ANOTHER UNION RISK:

THE UNION CAN CALL YOU OUT ON STRIKE

WHAT COULD HAPPEN IF NEGOTIATIONS BREAK DOWN
AND YOU ARE CALLED OUT ON STRIKE?

FOR NO STRIKE RISK,
VOTE NO

Day 15

SUPERVISORY HANDOUT

YOUR PERSONAL STRIKE COST CALCULATOR

HOW LONG WILL IT TAKE YOU TO BREAK EVEN AFTER
A FOUR-WEEK STRIKE?

STRIKE COST CALCULATOR				
IF YOU WORK 40 HOURS PER WEEK, AND YOUR PAY IS:	DURING A 4-WEEK STRIKE, YOUR TOTAL LOST WAGES ARE:	IF YOU GOT *NO* SALARY INCREASE AS A RESULT OF A STRIKE	IT WILL TAKE YOU THIS LONG TO BREAK EVEN IF, *BECAUSE OF THE STRIKE* YOU GET AN INCREASE OF:	
			$0.10	$0.20
$320 ($8/HOUR)	$1,280.00	YOU	6 YEARS 8 WEEKS	3 YEARS 4 WEEKS
		NEVER		
$360 ($9/HOUR)	$1,440.00	MAKE UP	6 YEARS 48 WEEKS	3 YEARS 24 WEEKS
$400 ($10/HOUR)	$1,600.00	THE LOST	7 YEARS 36 WEEKS	3 YEARS 44 WEEKS
$440 ($11/HOUR)	$1,760.00	WAGES	8 YEARS 24 WEEKS	4 YEARS 12 WEEKS
		IF YOU ARE NOT PERMANENTLY REPLACED		

AN ECONOMIC STRIKE COULD BE VERY COSTLY FOR
YOU AND YOUR FAMILY

CHAPTER XVII

FINAL WEEK OF THE CAMPAIGN

The campaign continues. The final week is the most critical. Both the employer and the union intensify their efforts. The union accelerates its home visits and calls mass meetings. The employer meets frequently with supervisors and encourages their active participation. In the final days before the election there are a number of details which require attention. The "Checklist for Final Week," at page 198, helps avoid overlooking important items during this often hectic time.

DAY 16

POSTING NOTICE

At least one week before the election, the employer should receive from the Board's regional office several copies of the official Notice of Election reproduced at page 199. If the notices do not arrive by that time, the Board should be notified. The notices must be posted conspicuously in the facility at least three full business days prior to the date of the election and should be protected against defacement. If someone marks one of the choices on the sample ballot reproduced on the notice, a clean notice should be substituted. However, defacement of the notice is not a basis for challenging the election's validity. *Brookville Healthcare Ctr.* (1993).

DAY 17

HOME MAILING

As momentum builds toward the election, the employer will emphasize its commitment to a progressive and responsible employee relations program in a final home mailing. The letter illustrated at page 200 clearly contrasts the stability of such a program with the risks of strikes.

SUPERVISORY HANDOUT

Employees should be reminded of the dilemma they would face in the event of a strike—picket or be fined, work or be replaced. The handout "A Striker's Choice: Picket or Be Fined," reproduced at page 201, lists some facts of life during a strike.

"VOTE NO" BUTTONS

Employers may make available "Vote No" buttons by leaving them around the premises, such as on a table near the time clock. Supervisors may wear the buttons, prompting employees to ask for one. *If asked*, the supervisor can give an employee a button, but the employer improperly interferes with the election when supervisors distribute buttons unsolicited.

DAY 18

SUPERVISORY MEETING

The employer should meet with all supervisors to share feedback and develop responses to any new issues or questions. Supervisors should be warned not to hold meetings with two or more employees within twenty-four hours of the balloting (See discussion at Day 19). This rule does not prevent campaigning with individual employees and supervisors should be advised they can continue one-on-one discussions with employees up to and including election day.

As with political campaigns, a high voter turnout is desirable. The employer should know which employees will be absent on election day and, if advantageous, furnish them with transportation or reimburse them for actual travel expenses. Making these arrangements is lawful if the offer is available to all employees. Another check of absentees should be made on the morning of the election, and transportation offered them.

Caution

Offering employees not scheduled to work on election day additional compensation to come to vote is a ground for setting aside the election. *Sunrise Rehabilitation Hosp.* (1995).

DAY 19

GROUP PRESENTATION

The employer should make a final presentation to employees in a large group setting. A high-level management representative—possibly one who has not participated directly in the communications campaign—may be chosen to deliver the message. The talk should focus on the campaign issues of greatest concern to the employees and, if possible, be very motivational.

In addition, a separate voting demonstration with "role playing" may be given. Employees who have never participated in a Labor Board election may be apprehensive about doing so. An explanation of the procedure familiarizes these employees with the process while also minimizing the possibility of improperly marked and void ballots. A sample script is provided at pages 202 and 203.

Caution

(The 24-Hour Rule)

In *Peerless Plywood Co.* (1953), the Board established a rule prohibiting election speeches by either party, union or employer, on company time to massed assemblies of employees within the 24 hours before an election. The rationale for the rule was that such speeches, because of their timing, gave an unfair advantage to the party who obtained the last word within the 24 hours. See *Bro-Tech Corp.* (1994). If employee attendance at the meeting is voluntary and on the employee's own time, the 24-hour rule does not apply. The voluntary meeting can be on or off company premises and it may include a meal.

Since an employer is bound by the actions of its supervisors, a mandatory employee meeting with their supervisor (or leadman with apparent authority) addressing union topics within 24 hours would violate the rule. Violation of the 24-hour rule automatically results in a second election, if timely objections are filed.

SUPERVISORY HANDOUT

The voting demonstration also presents an opportunity to distribute a sample ballot. It may be copied from the Board's official ballot, which appears in the middle section of the Notice of Election reproduced at page 199. Reproduction and distribution of the Board's official ballot, accompanied by the employer's editorial comments, is permissible when it is clear that the employer has added the comments. (See **Illustration** at page 204).

DAY 20

On election day supervisors may continue to have individual conversations with employees away from the polling area. If desired, a handout may be distributed. Election-day activities are discussed more fully in the next chapter.

Day 16

CHECKLIST FOR FINAL WEEK

__ Select employees willing to serve as election observer(s).

__ Arrange to pay company observers for time spent during the election. (You may pay the company observer and not pay the union observer.)

__ Post Notice of Election at least three full business days preceding election day and cover the notices with clear plastic so no marking can be made on them.

__ Have a handout in reserve for election day, if necessary.

__ Prepare an amended *Excelsior* list, if necessary.

__ Arrange an election morning check of absentees and bring them in to vote, if desirable.

__ Conduct final discussions with supervisors and remind them of the 24-hour rule. (They may continue individual campaigning and should encourage employees to vote.)

__ Instruct supervisors to keep away from the polling area during the election.

__ Plan the route for escorting union representatives to the pre-election conference to avoid disturbing production or exposing employees to them.

__ Arrange to remove posted campaign literature near the voting area on the day of the election.

__ Give instructions to observers, inform them of potential challenges and give them a list of names to be challenged. Instruct them not to sign the certification of conduct of election.

__ Prepare a letter to employees about the results of the election (see the illustration in Chapter XIX at page 229 for a sample letter).

DAY 16

UNITED STATES OF AMERICA ★ NATIONAL LABOR RELATIONS BOARD
NOTICE OF ELECTION

29-RC-8769 (RD DIR)

VOTING UNIT

INCLUDED:

EXCLUDED:

TIME AND PLACE OF ELECTION

DATE: WEDNESDAY, MARCH 12, 1997   TIME: 4:00 A.M. TO 6:30 A.M.
2:00 P.M. TO 4:00 P.M.

PLACE:

GENERAL

PURPOSE OF THIS ELECTION — This election is to determine the representative, if any, desired by the eligible Employees for purposes of collective bargaining with their Employer (See VOTING UNIT in this Notice of Election for description of eligible employees.) A majority of the valid ballots cast will determine the results of the election.

SECRET BALLOT — The election will be by SECRET ballot under the supervision of the Regional Director of the National Labor Relations Board. Voters will be allowed to vote without interference, restraint, or coercion. Electioneering will not be permitted at or near the polling place. Violations of these rules should be reported immediately to the Board agent or agent in charge of the election. Your attention is called to Section 12 of the National Labor Relations Act.

ANY PERSON WHO SHALL WILLFULLY RESIST, PREVENT, IMPEDE, OR INTERFERE WITH ANY MEMBER OF THE BOARD OR ANY OF ITS AGENTS OR AGENCIES IN THE PERFORMANCE OF DUTIES PURSUANT TO THIS ACT SHALL BE PUNISHED BY A FINE OF NOT MORE THAN $5,000 OR BY IMPRISONMENT FOR NOT MORE THAN ONE YEAR, OR BOTH.

Upon arrival at the voting place, voters should proceed to the Board agent and identify themselves by stating their name. The Board agent will hand a ballot to each eligible voter. Voters will enter the voting booth that constitutes the polling place, mark the ballot DO NOT SIGN YOUR BALLOT, fold the ballot before leaving the voting booth, then personally deposit it in a ballot box under the supervision of the Board agent and leave the polling area.

A sample of the official ballot is shown at the center of this Notice

ELIGIBILITY RULES — Employees eligible to vote are those described under VOTING UNIT in this Notice of Election, including employees who did not work during the designated payroll period because they were ill or on vacation or temporarily laid off, and also including employees in the military service of the United States who appear in person at the polls. Employees who have quit or been discharged for cause since the designated payroll period and who have not been rehired or reinstated prior to the date of this election are not eligible to vote.

SPECIAL ASSISTANCE — Any employee or other participant in this election who has a handicap and who in order to participate in this election needs special assistance such as a sign language interpreter, should notify the Regional Director as soon as possible and request the necessary assistance.

CHALLENGE OF VOTERS — If your eligibility to vote is challenged, you will be allowed to vote a challenged ballot. Although you may believe you are eligible to vote, the polling area is not the place to resolve the issue. Give the Board agent your name and any other information you are asked to provide. After you receive a ballot, proceed to the voting booth, mark your ballot and fold it so as to keep the mark secret. DO NOT SIGN YOUR BALLOT. Return to the Board agent who will ask you to place your ballot in a challenged envelope, seal the envelope, place it in the ballot box and leave the polling area. Your eligibility will be resolved later.

AUTHORIZED OBSERVERS — Each of the interested parties may designate an equal number of observers, this number to be determined by the Regional Director or agent in charge of the election. These observers (a) act as checkers at the voting place and at the counting of ballots; (b) assist in the identification of voters, (c) challenge voters and ballots, and (d) otherwise assist the Regional Director or agent.

INFORMATION CONCERNING ELECTION — The Act provides that only one valid representation election may be held in a 12-month period. Any employee who desires to obtain any further information concerning the terms and conditions under which this election is to be held, or who desires to raise any question concerning the holding of an election, the voting unit, or eligibility rules, may do so by communicating with the Regional Director or agent in charge of the election.

RIGHTS OF EMPLOYEES

Under the National Labor Relations Act, employees have the right

* To self-organization
* To form, join, or assist labor organizations
* To bargain collectively through representatives of their own choosing
* To act together for the purpose of collective bargaining or other mutual aid or protection
* To refuse to do any or all of these things unless the Union and Employer, in a State where such agreements are permitted, enter into a lawful union-security agreement requiring employees to pay periodic dues and initiation fees. Nonmembers who inform the union that they object to the use of their payments for nonrepresentational purposes may be required to pay only their share of the union's costs of representational activities (such as collective bargaining, contract administration and grievance adjustment).

It is the responsibility of the National Labor Relations Board to protect employees in the exercise of these rights.

The Board wants all eligible voters to be fully informed about their rights under Federal law and wants both Employers and Unions to know what is expected of them when it holds an election.

If agents of either Unions or Employer interfere with your right to a free, fair, and honest election, the election can be set aside by the Board. When appropriate the Board provides other remedies, such as reinstatement for employees fired for exercising their rights, including backpay from the party responsible for their discharge.

The following are examples of conduct that interfere with the rights of employees and may result in the setting aside of the election:

* Threatening loss of jobs or benefits by an Employer or a Union
* Promising or granting promotions, pay raises or other benefits to influence an employee's vote by a party capable of carrying out such promises
* An Employer firing employees to discourage or encourage union activity or a Union causing them to be fired to encourage union activity
* Making campaign speeches to assembled groups of employees on company time within the 24-hour period before the election
* Incitement by either an Employer or a Union of racial or religious prejudice by inflammatory appeals
* Threatening physical force or violence to employees by a Union or an Employer to influence their votes

The National Labor Relations Board protects your right to a free choice

Improper conduct will not be permitted. All parties are expected to cooperate fully with the National Labor Relations Board in maintaining basic principles of a fair election as required by law. The National Labor Relations Board as an agency of the United States Government does not endorse any choice in the election

NATIONAL LABOR RELATIONS BOARD
an agency of the
UNITED STATES GOVERNMENT

WARNING: THIS IS THE ONLY OFFICIAL NOTICE OF THIS ELECTION AND MUST NOT BE DEFACED BY ANYONE. ANY MARKINGS THAT YOU MAY SEE ON ANY SAMPLE BALLOT OR ANYWHERE ON THIS NOTICE HAVE BEEN MADE BY SOMEONE OTHER THAN THE NATIONAL LABOR RELATIONS BOARD, AND HAVE NOT BEEN PUT THERE BY THE NATIONAL LABOR RELATIONS BOARD. THE NATIONAL LABOR RELATIONS BOARD IS AN AGENCY OF THE UNITED STATES GOVERNMENT, AND DOES NOT ENDORSE ANY CHOICE IN THE ELECTION.

DAY 17

HOME MAILING

Dear Fellow Employee:

As you know, on Friday an election will be held to determine whether or not you will be represented by the union.

The basic issue is whether to continue to work under the philosophy and policies which have been the cornerstone of our good relations with you over the years or abandon them and substitute the unknown and often risky policies of outside union officials.

OUR UNION-FREE APPROACH

We believe each and every employee deserves to be treated with dignity and respect. We also believe in providing fair wages and know you are entitled to peace of mind with regard to your family's needs in the event of misfortune. And we believe in a fringe benefit program that includes company-paid health insurance, life insurance, retirement, profit sharing, holidays, and vacations. We have provided these benefits without the need for a union and the obligations unions impose upon their members.

UNION RISKS

By now, you have heard a lot about the many risks of unionization, including union strikes. WE NEVER WANT TO FACE THOSE RISKS HERE. NO ONE WINS IN A STRIKE. Unfortunately, many union members have learned that lesson the hard way.

We hope you will reject this bid by the union for your membership—and your dues. We respectfully ask for your support. Ours has been a sincere effort over the years to make your company the finest possible place to work. We will continue our efforts. You can help us—and help yourself—by voting NO.

Sincerely,

DAY 17

SUPERVISORY HANDOUT

A STRIKER'S CHOICE: PICKET OR BE FINED

- Strikers get no regular paycheck or company paid benefits, although regular bills continue.
- Strikes often involve violence and intimidation.
- If you try to work to help support your family and cross a picket line, the union can *fine* you hundreds of dollars.
- If you do not pay your union fine, the union may drag you into court to collect.
- Economic strikers are not guaranteed a job when and if the strike ends. They can be permanently replaced and may return to work only if an opening occurs.

CAN *YOU* AFFORD THIS RISK?

DAY 19

VOTING DEMONSTRATION

We have written you several times about the vote that will finally take place on Friday. The voting process is not very complicated, but I want you to understand what will happen and what procedure you should follow.

I'd like you to join me in a little "role playing." I need three volunteers. How about you, Joe, you, John, and you, Mary. Mary, you act as the NLRB representative. Please sit at the table where the sign says "NLRB." John, you be the company observer. Please sit where the sign says "Company Observer." Joe, you will be the union observer. Please sit in front of the sign, "Union Observer." John and Joe are going to help the NLRB representative to make sure everyone who is eligible will receive a ballot to vote. I need two more observers who will stand by the ballot box and the voting booth to see that everything goes okay. Now, I need one more volunteer—Margaret, how about you? Will you please act the part of the "voter?"

As you know, the balloting will be from 8 to 9 a.m. and 3 to 4 p.m. in the stock room. The NLRB representative will come in early with a brand new ballot box. The representative will open it up and will demonstrate that there is nothing in it. (Hold up a cardboard box with a slot.) The Labor Board is very particular in seeing that everything is honest. The ballot box will be assembled only after it has been examined and before any vote is cast, so that everyone can be sure it is empty.

Margaret, you are the first in line to vote. You state your name to Mary. It will be checked against a list of those eligible to vote. The list has been prepared by the Company from its payroll. Now Margaret will be given a ballot (hold up sample ballot reproduced from the election notice)—just like this ballot. This is marked "sample." The ballot you get on Friday will be about this size but probably a different color.

The real observers will receive instructions from the Board agent on Friday. They may raise questions about whether someone seeking to vote is an employee or is eligible to vote. That person nevertheless will get a ballot and will vote under challenge. The challenged ballot is voted in secret like the other ballots, but it is first put into an envelope. The envelope is sealed and then it is put into the ballot box. Then, after the election, if there are enough challenged ballots to change the results, the Labor Board decides whether the person is eligible to vote and the vote counted.

I want to emphasize one very important point about marking the ballot. If you want the union, mark an "X" in the left box; if you do not want the union, mark an "X" in the right box, marked "No."

Do not put any mark on the ballot except an "X." If you do, it may be disqualified and thrown out. And don't sign your name. Just put an "X" in the box. If you make a mistake or have any questions about voting, ask the NLRB representative who will help you.

You see we have constructed a voting booth with a drop cloth curtain and a shelf. The Labor Board will probably bring along a portable one for the election. There will be a pencil in the booth. Now, take the ballot into the booth, Margaret.

After you mark the ballot in the booth, you fold the ballot over just once, with the "X" marked on the inside and put it into the ballot box. Margaret, where are you? You can come out now, Margaret!

As you can see, your vote is a secret one and known only to you. Don't let anyone tell you otherwise. The polls are closed at 4 p.m. Then the ballot box will be opened. The ballots will be taken out by the NLRB representative and counted. The results will be known right then and there.

Your supervisor will have a sample ballot for you to keep. It is exactly like the one on the Notice of Election. Look it over. If you have any questions, please feel free to ask your supervisor or come directly to me. Be sure to vote.

How about a big hand for our volunteers!

DAY 19

SUPERVISORY HANDOUT

BE SURE TO VOTE!

REMEMBER THE ELECTION ARRANGEMENTS:

DATE: JANUARY 29

PLACE: STOCK ROOM

TIME: 8 A.M. TO 9 A.M.

              3 P.M. TO 4 P.M.

THE BALLOT WILL LOOK LIKE THIS:

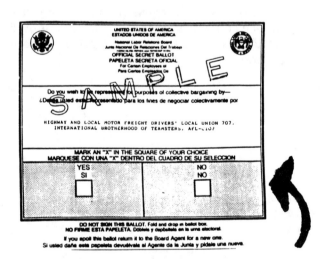

Your "X" in this square of the official ballot will mean *YOU DO NOT WANT THIS UNION.*

Distributed for your information by: (Employer's name)

CHAPTER XVIII

ELECTION DAY

Election day has finally arrived!

A number of days before the election, the Labor Board will have mailed the parties a form for designating observers and will have included written instructions concerning their duties (see **Illustration No. 35** at page 211). Each side is entitled to have an equal number of non-supervisory employees (one or two) to observe the balloting. The use of a supervisor as an observer may result in the Board's setting aside the election. *Bosart Co.* (1994). It is advisable to review the Board's instructions with the employer's observer before the balloting and give specific instructions on any challenges he or she should make on behalf of the employer. The observer should be advised to be certain to cast his or her ballot as well.

Approximately one-half hour before the polls open, the Board agent normally will hold a preelection conference with management and union representatives at the company premises. (The employer should arrange to escort the union representatives to the conference to avoid any last-minute union campaigning.) The observers will be called to attend the conference, be given identifying badges to wear ("Company Observer" or "Union Observer"), and instructed by the Board agent on their duties. Observers may keep a list of voters they intend to challenge, but they may not keep a list of employees who voted. *Masonic Homes of Cal., Inc.* (1981).

Most regional Board offices provide a portable aluminum voting booth with a curtained entrance. The Board agent will also bring a ballot box, which he or she will construct in front of the observers and the parties' representatives.

The Board agent will produce the list of eligible voters. This is the so-called *Excelsior* list the employer mailed to the Board for the union's use. Any objection concerning the list's completeness or accuracy probably would have been raised by the union when it received the list, but if not, the union may raise an objection at this time.

If the employer wants to change the voter eligibility list, it should have submitted an amended list to the Board prior to election day. This reduces the likelihood of union objections at the conference. Employees who have resigned or have been discharged prior to election day are not entitled to vote; the *Excelsior* list should be amended accordingly during the conference.

TWO-UNION CONTESTS AND RUN-OFF ELECTIONS

On occasion, two unions contend for representation rights among the same group of employees. The employer may lawfully express a preference for one or for neither in its campaign communications. If the employer expresses a preference, it may not do so in a manner that threatens employees or promises that it will act differently depending on the employees' choice. *Amboy Care Ctr.* (1996).

Arranging an election with two unions is the same as with one, except for the placement of the voting choices on the ballot. The "neither" designation is always in the center. Usually, the unions agree on their ballot placements; if not, they decide by flipping a coin.

If none of the choices (including "neither") receives a majority of the votes, a second election must be held. This is called a runoff election. The choices receiving the largest and second-largest number of votes participate in the runoff. Thus, the vote may be between two unions or for or against one of them. Only one runoff election may be held. The procedures involved in holding the runoff are like the original election. This time, of course, there is no "neither" choice.

There is an anomaly in a two-union runoff. If each of the two unions receives the same number of votes, neither one wins. The result is as if a majority of employees had voted against representation.

CONDUCTING THE ELECTION

Activity at or near the Polls

The Labor Board prohibits electioneering at or near the polls. Prolonged conversations between company or union officials and employees in the polling area are grounds for setting aside an election *regardless of what is discussed. Milchem, Inc.* (1968).

The Board has no definite rule establishing the distance from the polling area in which electioneering is prohibited. Each case is determined on its own facts. The presence of supervisors near the polling area without any conversation may interfere with the election and warrant setting it aside. In *Belk's Dep't Store* (1952), the Board stated:

> We are also convinced that, even though the supervisors were at some distance from the actual polling place, and apparently said nothing calculated to restrain or coerce the employees, their presence in the area where the employees were gathered while waiting to vote tended to interfere with the employees' freedom of choice of a bargaining agent.

In another case, a supervisor stationed himself in a walkway 10 to 15 feet from the entrance to the voting area. Though he was within the area of the plant where he worked, the Board set aside the election. *Electric Hose & Rubber Co.* (1982).

Opening the Polls

A few minutes before the polls open, the Board agent will direct everyone except the observers to leave. No management or union representatives may remain in or near the voting area during the balloting.

The employees coming to vote state their names and the observers verify their identity, checking off the names on the *Excelsior* eligibility list. The Board agent hands each employee a ballot which the employee takes into the voting booth. He or she marks a choice, folds the ballot, and drops it into the ballot box before leaving the booth.

In most elections, employees can vote any time between the opening and closing of the polls. Since elections usually take place at the worksite during work time, this may disrupt business, especially when there are many voters. Arrangements can be made between the parties, with the Board agent's concurrence, to stagger the voting by departments at predetermined times or by announcement over a public address system. Supervisors must not maintain lists indicating which employees have gone to the polling area.

Challenging Voters

The eligibility of a voter may be challenged either by an election observer or by the Board representative. The challenge must be made before the ballot is placed in the box. A later challenge is ineffectual. *Laidlaw Transit, Inc.* (1997).

Challenged voters put their marked ballots in a special envelope with a perforated stub. The Board agent writes the voter's name on the stub, along with the reason for the challenge and who is making it. The voter then puts the ballot into the envelope with the stub and deposits it into the ballot box.

There are various reasons why a voter may be challenged. He or she might be a supervisor or manager, not in a job classification included in the voting unit, a relative of the company's owner, retired or not on the *Excelsior* list.

If an individual is not on the eligibility list because of a termination that he or she claims was related to union activities, the voter will be given a ballot, even though no unfair labor practice charge had been filed. The person will then vote, but the ballot will be challenged by the Board agent or the employer observer.

Employees engaged in an economic strike who may have been permanently replaced are eligible to vote, providing the election is held within twelve months after the strike began. See 29 U.S.C. § 159(c)(3) (1995); *Bio-Science Lab. v. NLRB* (9th Cir. 1976).

Closing the Polls

The polls remain open until the time designated for closing. An employee who arrives late will not be permitted to vote absent "extraordinary circumstances." This has been held to mean a showing that one of the parties to the election was responsible for the employee's tardiness. *Monte Vista Disposal Co.* (1992).

When the polls close, the observers are asked to sign a "Certification on Conduct of Election" (see **Illustration No. 36** at page 212). This certifies that the balloting was conducted fairly, that all eligible voters were given an opportunity to cast their ballots in secret, and that the ballot box was protected in the interest of a fair and secret vote.

Caution

The Board agent usually obtains the observers' signatures before the employer representative has had an opportunity to consult with the employer's observer. Premature certification that the election was conducted fairly could prejudice the employer's position on any objections it may later file.

Before the balloting, the company observer should be instructed not to sign anything until he or she consults with the employer representative so that the observer can relate whether anything improper occurred during the balloting. For example, there may have been disturbances in the voting area, prolonged conversations between the union observer and voters, or failure to seal the ballot box. If conduct of this kind occurred, the observer should be instructed not to sign the certification form.

Counting the Ballots

After the polls close, the Board representative empties the ballot box and counts the ballots in the presence of the observers, company, and union personnel, who are permitted to return to the voting area.

The ballot count is always a tense moment. During the past weeks, the union and company have engaged in intensive campaigning. Now they are face to face. Whose efforts have been rewarded?

The ballot count may proceed in one of two ways. The ballots may be opened and placed face down on a table. Then, one by one, they are turned over and the "YES" votes and "NO" votes are called out. Another method is to separate the ballots into stacks of "YES" votes and "NO" votes. Once separated, they are counted and secured in stacks of fifty. With either method each person in the room keeps his or her own tally as the count proceeds.

Finally, all ballots are counted. The results are announced. The election is over.

Completing the Tally of Ballots

The Board agent will now complete a Tally of Ballots form (see **Illustration No. 37** at page 213). First, he will enter the approximate number of eligible voters, although this figure is not significant because the outcome is based on a majority of those who have voted.

Then, the number of votes cast for and against the union is entered. (Note that the sixth item on the tally of ballots does not read "votes cast for the employer!") Challenged and void ballots also are counted and entered. These numbers should equal the total number of names checked off on the eligibility list by the observers.

If the number of challenged ballots is not enough to affect the outcome, they have no significance and are destroyed. If the number is large enough to affect the outcome, the Board representative will try to gain the agreement of the parties to withdraw the challenges and open the ballots. If this fails, formal Board procedures come into play.

The union must have a majority of valid votes cast to win. If there are no challenges, a tie vote results in a loss for the union. If there are challenged ballots and, after the challenges are resolved, the vote also is tied, the union loses.

Caution

After the Board agent completes the Tally of Ballots, the observers are asked to sign it. Usually there is no reason for them not to sign. However, if the employer believes the count was inaccurate, improperly conducted, or certain ballots were improperly included or excluded, the company observer should be instructed not to sign it, since signing a certification of propriety could constitute a waiver of employer objections. A copy of the tally is then furnished to the parties.

After the tally of ballots has been completed, the election process is over. The Board representative disassembles the voting booth, picks up the empty box, collects the ballots, and leaves.

The Union's Departure

It is also time for the union representative to leave. Often, the representative is an "old hand" at the business and has won and lost many elections. As a professional, he or she usually will not express any words of bitterness about losing but may comment, "See you next year" or "You'll be hearing from us." The representative's reaction may provide a clue whether the union plans to file objections to the election. The basis for filing objections and the procedures for doing so are discussed in the following chapter.

ILLUSTRATION NO. 35

FORM NLRB-722
(7-89)

UNITED STATES OF AMERICA

NATIONAL LABOR RELATIONS BOARD

INSTRUCTIONS TO ELECTION OBSERVERS

DUTIES *(General)*:

1. Act as checkers and watchers.
2. Assist in identification of voters.
3. Challenge voters and ballots.
4. Otherwise assist Board Agents.

THINGS TO DO *(Specific)*:

1. Identify voter.
2. Check off the name of the person applying to vote. One check before the name by one organization. One check after the name by the other organization of the Company.
3. See that only one voter occupies a booth at any one time.
4. See that each voter deposits a ballot in the ballot box.
5. See that each voter leaves the voting room immediately after depositing ballot.
6. Report any conflict as to the right to vote to the Board Agent at your table.
7. Remain in the voting place until all ballots are counted in order to check on the fairness of the count, if ballots are counted at the time. If they are not counted immediately, you will be informed as to when and where ballots will be counted.
8. Report any irregularities to the Board Agent as soon as noticed.
9. Challenge of Voters - A Board Agent or an authorized observer may question eligibility of a voter. Such challenge **MUST** be made before the voter's ballot has been placed in the ballot box.
10. Wear your observer badge at all times during the conduct of the election.
11. BE ON TIME. *(One-half hour before the time for the opening of the polls.)*

THINGS NOT TO DO *(Specific)*:

1. Give any help to any voter. Only a Board Agent can assist the voter.
2. Electioneer any place during the hours of the election.
3. Argue regarding the election.
4. Leave the polling place without the Board Agent's consent.
5. Use intoxicating beverages.
6. Keep any list of those who have or have not voted.

As an official representative of your organization, you should enter upon this task with a fair and open mind. Conduct yourself so that no one can find fault with your actions during the election. You are here to see that the election is conducted in a fair and impartial manner, so that each eligible voter has a fair and equal chance to express himself/herself freely and in secret.

NATIONAL LABOR RELATIONS BOARD

ILLUSTRATION NO. 36

PM NLRB-750
7-681

UNITED STATES OF AMERICA
NATIONAL LABOR RELATIONS BOARD

CERTIFICATION ON CONDUCT OF ELECTION

Name of employer _____ Case No. _____

Date of election _____ Place _____

The undersigned acted as agents of the Regional Director and as authorized observers, respectively, in the conduct of the balloting at the above time and place.

WE HEREBY CERTIFY that such balloting was fairly conducted, that all eligible voters were given an opportunity to vote their ballots in secret, and that the ballot box was protected in the interest of a fair and secret vote.

For   **For the Regional Director, Region** _____

_____   _____

_____   _____

_____   _____

_____   _____

_____   _____

For   **For**

_____   _____

_____   _____

_____   _____

_____   _____

_____   _____

ILLUSTRATION NO. 37

FORM NLRB-760
(12-82)

UNITED STATES OF AMERICA
NATIONAL LABOR RELATIONS BOARD

Date Filed

Case No

Date Issued

**Type of Election
(Check one:)**

Stipulation
Board Direction
Consent Agreement
RD Direction
Incumbent Union *(Code)*

**(If applicable check
either or both:)**

8(b) (7)
Mail Ballot

TALLY OF BALLOTS

The undersigned agent of the Regional Director certifies that the results of the tabulation of ballots cast in the election held in the above case, and concluded on the date indicated above, were as follows

1 Approximate number of eligible voters
2 Number of Void ballots
3 Number of Votes cast for
4 Number of Votes cast for
5 Number of Votes cast for
6 Number of Votes cast against particpating labor organization(s)
7 Number of Valid votes counted (sum of 3, 4, 5, and 6)
8 Number of Challenged ballots
9 Number of Valid votes counted plus challenged ballots (sum of 7 and 8)
10 Challenges are (not) sufficient in number to affect the results of the election
11 A majority of the valid votes counted plus challenged ballots (Item 9) has (not) been cast for

For the Regional Director

The undersigned acted as authorized observers in the counting and tabulating of ballots indicated above. We hereby certify that the counting and tabulating were fairly and accurately done, that the secrecy of the ballots was maintained, and that the results were as indicated above. We also acknowledge service of this tally.

For

For

For

For

CHAPTER XIX

POSTELECTION PROCEEDINGS

In most instances the losing party in the election will accept the results without protest. On occasion, the loser may decide to file objections to the election based on questionable conduct affecting the outcome, particularly where the results are close. In some elections the number of challenged ballots also may affect the outcome. In either event, there will be further proceedings to resolve the issues.

There are two types of objections to an election. One relates to the Board's *conduct of the election* and the other to conduct by one of the participants or a third party *affecting the results of the election*. For example, if the Board representative permitted electioneering in the voting area, this would support an objection to the *conduct of the election*. If the employer, without identifying itself, distributed an official NLRB sample ballot with an X marked in the "NO" box, this would support a union objection to *conduct affecting the results of the election*.

When objections to an election are filed, the Board measures the conduct objected to against its "laboratory conditions" standard:

> In election proceedings, it is the Board's function to *provide a laboratory in which an experiment may be conducted*, under conditions as nearly ideal as possible, to determine the uninhibited desires of the employees. . . . When . . . the standard drops too low, because of our fault . . . or that of others, the requisite laboratory conditions are not present and the experiment must be conducted over again. *General Shoe Corp.* (1948) (Emphasis added.)

In evaluating the interference resulting from specific conduct, the Board does not attempt to assess the actual effect of the conduct on the employees. It makes its decision on the basis of whether it believes the questioned conduct "tended to prevent" the free expression of the employees' choice. (See NLRB 53d Annual Report 48 (1988)).

Although the Board has set aside thousands of elections based on its laboratory conditions standard, it has never conducted a scientific study to determine why employees vote the way they do or to what extent improper conduct influences their choice. The reasons for not doing so probably lie in the uncertainty of trying to evaluate voter behavior.

A private study concluded that "there is little evidence of the validity of the Board's assumptions regarding the impact of unlawful campaign tactics on voting behavior." J. Getman, S. Goldberg & J. Herman, *Union Representation Elections: Law and Reality* 5 (1976). See also *Getman v. NLRB* (D.C. Cir. 1971) (". . . in over 30 years [the Board] has itself never engaged in the kind of much needed systematic empirical effort to determine the dynamics of an election campaign or the type of conduct which actually has a coercive impact."). Nor has the Board engaged in such a survey in the most recent quarter of a century.

GENERAL STANDARDS

In order to serve as a basis for overturning an election, the conduct must have occurred during the "critical period," i.e. the period between the date the petition was filed and the date the election was held, *Ideal Elec. & Mfg. Co.* (1961), except in the case of a union's pre-petition offer to waive initiation fees. *Gibson Discount Ctr.* (1974).

As a general proposition, unfair labor practices committed during the critical period will be deemed to be objectionable conduct warranting the election to be set aside. However, "the criteria applied in determining whether certain conduct interfered with an election are not identical to the criteria applied in determining whether an unfair labor practice has been committed . . . ." *Kutsher's Country Club, Corp.* (1971). Therefore, not every unlawful act will overturn an election. The Board may decide that the conduct, although technically unlawful, was not severe enough to influence employees' votes. See for example, *West Texas Equip. Co.* (1963), where the Board held a single interrogation and two suggestions that benefits may be lost, occurring more than four months prior to the election, were insufficient to cause the election to be set aside.

Conversely, not every act that overturns an election is an unfair labor practice. For example, an employer's statement that, if the union won the election, "the blacks would take over" was held not be to be an unfair labor practice, even though the Board stated that the remark "may well be grounds for setting an election aside." *Glazers Wholesale*

Drug Co. (1974). When assessing objections based on employer conduct, the Board does not take into consideration the Act's "free speech" provision, section 8(c), which is inapplicable to representation cases. *Kalin Constr. Co.* (1996).

In considering objections based on alleged misrepresentations in campaign literature, the Board leaves to the employees the task of evaluating campaign propaganda. The Board will not scrutinize the substance of a statement as to whether it was true, false, or misleading. However, it will set aside an election in the case of trickery, fraud, or forged documents which, because of the deceptive manner in which they were presented, render voters unable to recognize the forgery as partisan election propaganda. *Midland Nat'l Life Ins. Co.* (1982).

OBJECTIONAL CONDUCT

Examples of Union Misconduct

Certain union conduct may overturn an election if timely objections are filed by the employer. Examples are electioneering within the designated polling area, *Star Expansion Indus. Corp.* (1968), misuse or alteration of Board documents, *GAF Corp.* (1978), an offer to waive initiation fees only for employees who sign authorization cards before an election, *NLRB v. Savair Mfg. Co.* (U.S. 1973), the offer of a $5 gift certificate, *General Cable Corp.* (1968), or $100 cash for a pro-union vote, *Revco D.S. Inc. v. NLRB* (6th Cir. 1987). However, it is not objectionable for a union to reimburse an employee for transportation expenses incurred in voting. *Sunrise Rehabilitation Hosp.* (1995).

Threats and violence against non-union supporters will also overturn an election. *Professional Research, Inc.* (1975). However, where an open union supporter stated to another employee on his way to vote "you better get yourself a bullet proof vest," the Board and reviewing court held that the union supporter did not have the apparent authority to speak on behalf of the union and, therefore, was not its agent. The employer's objections were dismissed and the union certified. *Overnite Transp. Co. v. NLRB* (8th Cir. 1997).

A recent case involved a union's use of a sound truck on the day of the election. Parking the truck on the street adjacent to the plant, the union repeatedly broadcast two taped songs with pro-union lyrics which were heard throughout the plant. The verse of one song stated:

Let's hail the Teamsters Union and sing of it with pride
Remember Teamster members, your Union's by your side

As long as we're together, our numbers will increase and
This will be our motto: prosperity and peace

Now all for one and one for all is something you have heard
But when the Teamsters say it, the boys mean every word

So hail the Teamsters Union and shout it loud and clear
The Brotherhood of Teamsters will always be right here.

The union won the election, 35 to 30. The employer filed objections, asserting the taped music violated the Board's *Peerless Plywood* rule prohibiting captive audience speeches within 24 hours of the election. The Board overruled the objections, holding that the song did not constitute a campaign speech within the meaning of *Peerless Plywood* because it did not contain any specific campaign promises.

The court disagreed, holding that the lyrics, when set to music, appealed to the most visceral emotions of the workers. "If modern political campaigns have taught us anything, it is that this type of emotional rhetoric has a heavy impact upon the voter." The court denied enforcement and remanded to the Board for further proceedings and a more adequate explanation of its reasoning. *Bro-Tech Corp. v. NLRB* (3d Cir. 1997).

Examples of Employer Misconduct

Some forms of employer conduct will automatically overturn an election if a timely objection is filed. Examples include distributing a marked sample ballot as described above, *Allied Elec. Prods., Inc.* (1954), electioneering within the polling area, *Volt Technical Corp.* (1969), or failing to submit an accurate *Excelsior* (voter eligibility) list with the full names of the eligible employees. *North Macon Health Care Facility* (1995). An election also will be overturned if the employer addresses an assembly of employees on working time within twenty-four hours of opening the polls, *Peerless Plywood Co.* (1953), or if the employer changes the pay process during this period (unless the change was motivated by a legitimate business reason unrelated to the election). *Kalin Constr. Co.* (1996). It is also objectionable for an employer to organize an employee betting pool on the outcome of the election which enables the employer to ascertain how individuals are likely to cast their ballots. *Wellstream Corp.* (1994).

EMPLOYER CONDUCT WHILE OBJECTIONS OR CHALLENGES ARE PENDING

All challenges and objections must be resolved before the representation proceeding is concluded. While they are pending, the employer should not make changes in wages, benefits, work hours, or other conditions of employment. Such conduct may violate the Act even though motivated by economic considerations. See *Casa San Miguel* (1995); *Mike O'Connor Chevrolet* (1974), *enf. denied on other grounds* (8th Cir. 1975).

On the other hand, withholding a wage increase because the employees selected the union is also unlawful. According to the Board, an employer's legal duty during a representation proceeding "is to proceed as he would have done had the union not been on the scene." *Atlantic Forest Prods.* (1987). This rule, which also applies before the election, has trapped countless employers and has been criticized by the courts. One court has observed: "This, like much advice, is, of course, easier to give than to put into practice." *NLRB v. Otis Hosp.* (1st Cir. 1976). Another panel of the same court commented:

> We are not unsympathetic with an employer who, having decided to increase his employees' wages, finds himself trying to navigate a "perilous" course between the *Scylla* of a violation of the Act for granting a wage increase to his employees when a representation election is pending and the *Charybdis* of a violation of the Act for withholding such an increase when such an election is pending. His uncertain compass is the Board's rule to act "as he would if a union were not in the picture." *Sun Chem. Corp. v. NLRB* (1st Cir. 1977).

The Board's failure to formulate a clear standard on granting or withholding wage and benefit adjustments before or after an election has also been criticized by the U.S. Court of Appeals for the District of Columbia. In frustration, the court stated, "[W]e throw up our judicial hands . . . ." *Acme Die Casting v. NLRB* (D.C. Cir. 1996). Until the law is clarified, legal advice is critical. Counsel should carefully analyze the facts and the law of the particular circuit court jurisdiction.

Once the objections are resolved and the union certified, the employer's obligation to bargain commences, notwithstanding pending exceptions to the regional director's report. *Allstate Ins. Co.* (1978). Following certification, the employer may not unilaterally change terms or conditions of employment. For example, it may not discontinue a practice of granting annual wage increases, unless it has retained total discretion under a merit increase program. *Daily News of L.A. v. NLRB* (D.C. Cir. 1996), *cert. denied* (U.S. 1997).

CONDUCT BY PRO-UNION SUPERVISORS

As noted in Chapter XIII, authorization cards obtained through a supervisor's encouragement are "tainted" and may not be used by a union to support the 30% showing of interest required to file a petition. Similarly, pro-union activity by a supervisor in the campaign preceding the election may cause the election to be invalidated when the employer demonstrates that "the supervisor's conduct reasonably tended to have such a coercive effect on the employees that it was likely to impair their freedom of choice in the election." *Evergreen Healthcare, Inc. v. NLRB*, (6th Cir. 1997).

CONDUCT BY NON-PARTIES

Conduct by non-parties also may destroy the requisite laboratory conditions and void an election. For example, community-sponsored attacks on a union, *Utica-Herbrand Tool Div. of Kelsey-Hayes Co.* (1964), or the arrest of a union organizer at the polling place, *Great Atlantic & Pacific Tea Co.* (1958), have been the bases for setting aside a union loss.

PROCEDURE FOR FILING OBJECTIONS

Within seven calendar days after service of the tally of ballots following the election, any party may file a written statement of objections to the conduct of the election or conduct affecting the results of the election. The objections must be supported by a brief statement of the reasons. The regional director will serve a copy of the objections on each of the other parties to the election. However, as a matter of courtesy, the party filing the objections is expected to immediately serve a copy on the other party. The party whose conduct is objected to will be asked to answer the objections.

The seven-day time limit is strictly applied and must be observed even if there is no clear winner due to challenged ballots that ultimately could affect the results. If objections are not received by mail or facsimile on or before the seventh day, they will not be considered.

PROCEDURE FOR INVESTIGATING OBJECTIONS

When timely objections are filed, the regional director will begin an administrative investigation by instructing the objecting party to submit supporting evidence within seven days:

> Evidence should be in the form of affidavits, written statements, or documents. If the evidence cannot be submitted in written form, but is to be presented through witnesses with knowledge of the allegations set out in the objections, a short statement as to the evidence each witness will be able to furnish must be submitted by the above date. *Bob G. Lewis d/b/a Classic Courts* (1979).

The scope of the investigation initially is determined by the regional director. The director has the discretion to limit the investigation to the specific objections raised by the parties. However, if evidence is uncovered during the investigation that indicates the election may in some manner have been tainted, the regional director is not precluded from considering such conduct simply because it was not specifically alleged in the objections.

Caution—The Johnnie's Poultry Rule

An employer considering whether to file objections has little time to gather evidence and limited access to discovery. If the objections require evidence from employees, the employer's attorney should interview them.

To conduct an employee interview, the attorney first must provide the employee with a *Miranda*-type warning. Just as the police are required to inform people who are in custody of their constitutional rights before interrogating them (*Miranda v. Arizona* (U.S. 1966)), the Board takes the position that questioning employees is inherently coercive unless, at the outset: (1) the employer discloses the purpose of the interview; (2) assures the employee there will be no reprisals for refusal to cooperate; and (3) obtains the employee's permission to engage in the interview. In addition, the questioning must occur in a context free from employer hostility to union organization, must not itself be coercive in nature, and the questions must not exceed the legitimate purpose of the investigation by prying into other union matters, elicit information concerning an employee's subjective state of mind, or otherwise interfere with the employee's statutory rights. *Johnnie's Poultry Co.* (1964), *enf. denied on other grounds* (8th Cir. 1965).

Similarly, the *Johnnie's Poultry* safeguards must be adhered to when interviewing employees to defend against union-filed objections. In either case, the questioning must be relevant to the objections. See *Paymaster Oil Mill Co.* (1970), *enf'd per curiam* (5th Cir. 1971) (applying *Johnnie's Poultry* standards to representation as well as unfair labor practice proceedings).

Should the employer or its attorney fail to follow this procedure, the Board is quick to find a violation of the Act. The case of *Standard-Coosa-Thatcher, Inc.* (1981), *enf'd* (4th Cir. 1982), is typical of the Board's strict application of its rules. The company attorney failed to give assurance against reprisal to one of the 70 employees interviewed. The Board stated it would not excuse the attorney's failure, "whether by design or inadvertence," and ruled that the company had engaged in unlawful coercive interrogation.

The Board's volumes contain hundreds of cases in which attorneys have transgressed the *Johnnie's Poultry* safeguards. Indeed, the AFL-CIO has proposed that a violation be the basis for Board disciplinary sanction against the offending attorney (*Rules Governing Misconduct by Attorneys or Party Representatives*, 29 C.F.R Part 102 (1996)). The courts in general have upheld the Board's rulings, although some have declined to apply them in a *per se* fashion, favoring a "totality of the circumstances" test. See cases noted in *Bill Scott Oldsmobile* (1987).

REGIONAL DIRECTOR'S INVESTIGATION AND DETERMINATION

When objections are filed, the regional director will conduct an administrative investigation. If the director concludes the objections are not meritorious or do not raise substantial and material factual issues, the director will issue a report or supplemental decision dismissing the objections. If the regional director concludes the objections have merit or discovers other objectionable conduct, he or she may set the election aside. Alternatively, if the regional director concludes that the objections raise substantial and material factual issues, a hearing may be held to resolve those issues.

Practically speaking, the regional office conducts only a minimal investigation to determine the existence of such factual issues. Once it becomes apparent that there is a credibility dispute over material facts, most regions will stop investigating and set the case down for an evidentiary hearing. Indeed, even hearsay evidence may be sufficient to warrant setting the matter for hearing. This practice saves agency resources and avoids a remand by a court of appeals in a subsequent test of certification.

Where the balloting was held pursuant to a *stipulated agreement*, the Board, rather than the regional director, will make the final determination on the objections. The hearing officer prepares a report to the Board which resolves issues of credibility, makes finding of fact, and recommends whether the objections should be sustained. (This is in contrast to the preelection hearing to determine the appropriate unit, where the hearing officer may not make recommendations or findings.) The case is then transferred to the Board and the parties may file exceptions to the report with the Board.

Where the balloting was held pursuant to a *directed election*, the regional director reviews the hearing officer's report and exceptions. The director has the option of issuing a report or a supplemental decision. If a director issues a report, the parties have a right to file exceptions with the Board as in the case of a stipulated agreement. If the director issues a supplemental decision, Board review is secured through the filing of a request for review. The grounds upon which review will be granted are the same as those used in seeking Board review of the regional director's preelection unit determinations (see Chapter XV at page 151).

BOARD REVIEW

If a request for review has been granted or exceptions filed, the Board proceeds to resolve the outstanding issues. If the Board concludes that substantial and material factual issues do not exist, it may decide the case on the basis of the administrative record alone. If it concludes that substantial and material factual issues do exist, the Board may direct that a hearing be held before a hearing officer. At the conclusion of the hearing, the hearing officer will issue a written report resolving questions of credibility and containing recommendations regarding the disposition of all outstanding issues. The rules regarding the timely filing of exceptions, supporting briefs, and answering briefs are the same as those applicable to hearings ordered by the regional director.

If the Board or the regional director overrules the objections and the results of the election are otherwise conclusive, an appropriate certification will be issued. If the objections are sustained in whole or in part, the first election will be set aside and a rerun election directed, unless the case has been consolidated with an unfair labor practice case and the objectionable conduct is serious enough to warrant issuance of a bargaining order.

PROCEDURE FOR INVESTIGATING CHALLENGED BALLOTS

The same procedure is followed to resolve challenged ballots, which are usually considered at the same time as objections. If the number of challenged ballots is sufficient to affect the outcome of the election, the regional director will notify the parties after the election. A list of the names of the individuals challenged, their job titles, the identity of the party who challenged them, and the reason for the challenge is attached to the notice. The party making the challenge is given seven days to supply substantiating evidence. The other party is also asked to state and support its position.

If the regional director concludes as a result of the investigation that the challenges can be resolved more appropriately after testimony is taken, a hearing will be scheduled and a report will be prepared. Thereafter, the procedure is the same as the investigation of objections. If the regional director or the Board finds no merit to the challenges, the ballots are counted. The identifying perforated stubs are detached and the ballots are removed from the envelopes and mixed with the others to eliminate any possibility of identifying the challenged voters. A revised tally is issued and the results certified, provided there are no pending objections.

If the union loses the election (a majority of the votes cast are against union representation and the challenged ballots are insufficient in number to affect the results) and no objections are filed within the seven-day period, the regional director will issue a *Certification of Results of Election* (see **Illustration No. 38** at page 227). If the union wins the election, the regional director will issue a *Certification of Representative* (see **Illustration No. 39** at page 228). The proceeding is then closed.

RERUN ELECTIONS

When the regional director or the Board sets aside an election, a second or rerun election is held. The same procedures govern a rerun election: a conference is held to determine the time and place of voting; new notices are posted; and the parties appeal to the electorate for their vote. This time, however, there is a new campaign issue—the conduct that caused the Board to void the first election. If employer misconduct caused the election to be set aside, the union will exploit the employer's transgression. The employer may point out that, despite the union's objections, a majority of the employees voted against union representation. Management should stress the reasons the employees should again reject the union. Of course, it should avoid repeating the conduct that gave rise to the union's valid objections.

Conversely, if the union won the election and it is set aside based on the employer's objections, the employer has a second chance. It may capitalize on the union's misconduct that led to the new election. In any event, management should redouble its effort. In most instances, the outcome of the rerun is the same as the original election.

IF THE UNION WINS

Suppose the unlikely happens. Notwithstanding the employer's efforts, the union wins the contest. It is certified as the collective bargaining agent. What should the employer do?

Of course, management feels let down, but that should not lead to scorn, retribution, or vindictiveness. Management is still running the company. At the outset, the employer should write to the employees and acknowledge the results of the election. Then it must study its obligation to engage in collective bargaining.

The union is now the agent of the employees, and the employer may not bargain with employees in groups or individually. To do so would undermine the representation rights granted the union by law. However, it can still meet and communicate directly with the employees, as long as its actions do not interfere with the union's status as their collective bargaining representative.

In the overwhelming majority of cases, this will be the employer's last election. It will learn to live with the union as do the employers of some 16 million employees. We urge here, however, that the same effort expended in winning the election be used to win the peace.

Having opened up the gates of communication, the employer should keep them open. It should keep its employees informed of company plans and the progress of its negotiations with the union. It should strive to keep their good will and cooperation. There may come a day when management will again need their special support.

IF THE UNION LOSES

If the employer has done its utmost, it is likely that the union will not obtain a majority of the votes. The employer will be wrapped in the glow of victory. Many employers write letters to their employees to express their appreciation (see **Illustration No. 40** at page 229).

Following the certification of results, improved benefits and wage increases may be granted, preferably based upon some past timetable or other credible rationale. On occasion, the precipitous grant of wage increases and improved benefits (even after the certification of results) has been held unlawful as the fulfillment of earlier promises.

Now that the election is over, the employer feels safe for a year. There cannot be another election for twelve months from the day of the election. Management assumes the union has accepted defeat and turned its attention elsewhere. This is not necessarily the case. The twelve-month rule does not give complete insulation. During this period (and thereafter), the employer is susceptible to organizing efforts by either the defeated union or another labor organization. If either one signs up a majority of the employees, it is barred from seeking an election but is not barred from seeking recognition. The union may charge the employer with a refusal to bargain and, if it can meet the *Gissel* criteria discussed in Chapter XI, it may be well on the way toward an order to bargain. While this situation occurs rarely, it has happened.

An employer should not be lulled into a false sense of security. Twelve months pass quickly. Employees do not easily forget the campaign assertions. The union, too, will not forget. It may keep a watchful eye over the company, ready to exploit management's mistakes.

The employer's vigilance must be constant. It was awakened from its lethargy and prevailed, but it must continue to communicate. The talks, the explanations, the group meetings, the home mailings, and the supervisory communications must be maintained.

EPILOGUE

We have suggested steps toward a wholesome employee/employer relationship. Although we have not mentioned the Golden Rule, what has been outlined is its most important ingredient. Give employees trust and they will trust you. Speak to them and they will speak to you. Listen to them and they will listen to you. Follow these precepts and you may never have to face another union organizing campaign or NLRB election.

ILLUSTRATION NO. 38

FORM NLRB-4280
(1-66)

RC — RM — RD

UNITED STATES OF AMERICA
NATIONAL LABOR RELATIONS BOARD

Employer

and

Petitioner

TYPE OF ELECTION

(CHECK ONE)

☐ CONSENT

☒ STIPULATED

☐ RD DIRECTED

☐ BOARD DIRECTED

(ALSO CHECK BOX BELOW WHEN APPROPRIATE)

☐ *8(b)(7)*

CASE

CERTIFICATION OF RESULTS OF ELECTION

An election has been conducted under the Board's Rules and Regulations. The Tally of Ballots shows that no collective-bargaining representative has been selected. No timely objections have been filed.

As authorized by the National Labor Relations Board,

It is certified that a majority of the valid ballots have not been cast for any labor organization and that no labor organization is the exclusive representative of these employees in the bargaining unit described below:*

INCLUDED: All full-time and regular part-time salespersons, installer/technicians and stock persons employed by the Employer.

EXCLUDED: All office clerical employees, the store manager, the office manager, casual employees, all other employees of the Employer, and guards, professional employees and supervisors as defined by the Act.

Daniel Silverman

Signed at ____New York, New York____

On the ____20th____ day of

____June____ 1990

Regional Director, Region ___2___
National Labor Relations Board

UNITED STATES OF AMERICA

NATIONAL LABOR RELATIONS BOARD

RC — RM — RD

TYPE OF ELECTION
(CHECK ONE)
☐ CONSENT

☐ STIPULATED

☐ RD DIRECTED

☐ BOARD DIRECTED

CASE

(ALSO CHECK BOX
BELOW WHEN APPROPRIATE)

☐ 8(b)(7)

CERTIFICATION OF REPRESENTATIVE

An election has been conducted under the Board's Rules and Regulations. The Tally of Ballots shows that a collective-bargaining representative has been selected. No timely objections have been filed.

As authorized by the National Labor Relations Board, it is certified that a majority of the valid ballots have been cast for

and that it is the exclusive collective-bargaining representative of the employees in the following appropriate unit.

UNIT:

Signed at _____

On the _____ day of

_____ 19

Regional Director, Region _____
National Labor Relations Board

ILLUSTRATION NO. 40

Employer Letter:
Expression of Appreciation

Dear Fellow Employees:

The NLRB election is over and a majority of you decided against the union. I want to thank you sincerely for your support. We interpret the result as a strong mandate for the continuance of the policies which have made our company such a fine place to work.

With this election behind us, let's look to the future. Our mutual goals must be high: high efficiency, high cooperation, and high quality. By working together, our company can grow and furnish better jobs for all of us and greater rewards for our families.

Thanks again for your support. We will make every effort to justify it.

Sincerely,

General Manager

APPENDIX

GLOSSARY OF LABOR RELATIONS TERMS

ADMINISTRATIVE LAW JUDGE

An administrative officer of the National Labor Relations Board who presides at NLRB trials to determine if unfair labor practices have been committed.

AGENT

A person who is authorized by law to act for another person. For example, a supervisor is an "agent" of an employer.

APPROPRIATE UNIT

A group of employees sharing common interests who are eligible to vote together to decide if they want a union to represent them.

ARBITRATION

A method of deciding a dispute in which the parties to the dispute have agreed that an outside person or persons shall hear and decide the dispute.

ASSESSMENTS

A sum of money required by unions of their members for special purposes, such as strike contributions and special legal costs. Assessments are in addition to normal dues and initiation fees.

AUTHORIZATION CARD

A card signed by an employee designating a union as his or her representative for purposes of bargaining collectively with an employer. An authorization card may be used to support a petition for an election with the NLRB, a card check, a demand for recognition, or, where unfair labor practices have occurred, an order by the NLRB requiring an employer to recognize and bargain with a union.

BARGAINING IN GOOD FAITH

Generally means both sides must meet at reasonable times with a good faith intention of reaching a mutually acceptable agreement. Neither side, however, is required to adopt a contract proposal or make a concession so long as its bargaining obligation is carried out in good faith.

BARGAINING ORDER

An order by the NLRB that a company must recognize and bargain with a union.

BUSINESS AGENT OR REPRESENTATIVE

An official agent of the union who conducts its business of organizing, negotiating, or administering union matters.

CARD CHECK

A process of comparing signatures on union authorization cards against an employer's payroll records to determine whether a valid majority of employees have signed authorization cards.

CHARGE

An allegation against an employer or a union alleging that the National Labor Relations Act has been violated. Technically, an unfair labor practice charge.

CHECK-OFF CLAUSE

A contract clause which requires an employer to deduct union dues from the pay checks of employees for direct payment to the union.

COLLECTIVE BARGAINING CONTRACT

A formal agreement regarding wages, hours, and conditions of employment entered into between an employer and a union.

CONCERTED ACTIVITIES

Activities undertaken by two or more employees acting together or one employee acting on behalf of or as the representative of his co-workers. Where such concerted activities are undertaken by employees to improve their wages, hours, or working conditions, they are generally "protected" by law unless carried out by indefensible means such as violent or unlawful conduct.

DECERTIFICATION ELECTION

An election held by the NLRB to determine whether employees represented by a union no longer wish to be represented by a union.

DEMAND FOR RECOGNITION

A demand by a union that an employer recognize it as the representative of the company's employees, based upon signed authorization cards from a majority of the employees.

DISTRIBUTION

The distribution of advertising, handbills, literature, or other written or printed material (except union authorization cards). Employee distribution may be prohibited on "work time" and in "work areas." See also "Solicitation."

ECONOMIC STRIKE

Generally encompasses any strike by employees for improved wages, benefits, hours, or terms or conditions of employment. Most accurately, it is any strike other than one which is caused or prolonged by the unfair labor practices of an employer. Economic strikes usually involve disputes over the terms of a new collective bargaining agreement or the protection of working conditions.

FINES

Financial penalties by a union against members who violate its constitution, by-laws, or other rules. For example, fines can be imposed for crossing union picket lines, missing union meetings, "demeaning" union members, etc.

FREE SPEECH

The right of employers to express their views, arguments, and opinions with respect to unionization, which is specifically protected under section 8(c) of the National Labor Relations Act.

FRINGE BENEFITS

The terms used to describe employee compensation other than wages.

GRIEVANCE

A complaint by an employee or union that a provision of a collective bargaining agreement has been violated by an employer.

INITIATION FEES

A one-time payment required of an applicant to join a union.

INJUNCTION

An order by a court forbidding a person or party from engaging in prohibited activity, such as an unlawful strike.

INTERNATIONAL UNION

The term commonly applied to a parent union.

INTERROGATION

The questioning of an employee about his/her membership in, feelings about, or activity on behalf of a union or the membership, feelings, or activities of other employees.

LOCAL UNION

A union holding a charter from a national or international labor organization. Most local unions have defined geographical boundaries.

LOCKOUT

The closing down of part or all of a company by an employer in order to bring pressure upon employees to abandon their demands or to accept an employer's proposals.

MAJORITY STATUS

The term used to describe the status of a union which has obtained signed authorization cards from a majority of employees in an appropriate bargaining unit.

MANAGEMENT RIGHTS CLAUSE

A clause in a collective bargaining agreement which expressly preserves certain rights of management to run its business without union involvement or interference.

NATIONAL LABOR RELATIONS BOARD

The federal agency charged with regulating the relations between management, employees, and unions.

OBJECTIONABLE CONDUCT

Conduct which prevents the holding of a fair, secret ballot election and which usually requires a new election to be held.

OPEN SHOP

A unionized company which does not require employees to become a member of the union as a condition of continued employment.

ORGANIZING DRIVE

A campaign by a union to collect employee signatures on authorization cards.

PERMANENT REPLACEMENT

An employee hired by an employer to permanently replace an employee who is engaging in an economic strike.

PETITION

An official document requesting the NLRB to conduct a representation election.

REPRESENTATION CASE

The term used by the NLRB to describe an election proceeding before the Board.

REPRESENTATION ELECTION

A secret ballot election held by the NLRB to determine whether employees desire to have a union represent them.

RIGHT TO WORK LAWS

The term used to describe laws in several states which forbid unions and employers from entering into a collective bargaining agreement which requires employees to become a member of a union as a condition of employment.

SALTING

The practice by a union of having its members or organizers obtain employment with a non-union employer to organize its employers.

SHOP STEWARD

An employee designated by a union to represent its interests at a company.

SHOWING OF INTEREST

Evidence presented to the NLRB that at least 30% of the employees in an alleged appropriate bargaining unit desire that an election be held. Usually the showing of interest presented to the NLRB is in the form of union authorization cards.

SOLICITATION

Activities by a union or other group enlisting employee support. Solicitation describes all oral communication *and* the distribution of union authorization cards. Employee solicitation may be prohibited on "work time," i.e., when the employee is supposed to be actually working. See also "Distribution."

STRIKE

The concerted refusal of employees to work in order to bring pressure on a company to meet their demands.

STRIKE BENEFITS

Nominal payments sometimes made by a union to striking employees.

STRIKE REPLACEMENTS

A term used to describe employees hired (permanently or temporarily) to perform the jobs of employees out on strike.

SURVEILLANCE

Spying on an employee's activities on behalf of a union.

SYMPATHY STRIKE

Employees who respect a picket line established by another union are referred to as sympathy strikers.

TEMPORARY REPLACEMENT

An employee hired by an employer to replace a striking or locked-out employee only for the duration of the strike or lockout.

UNAUTHORIZED STRIKE

A strike by employees without the consent of their union. Also known as a "wildcat" or "unsanctioned" strike.

UNFAIR LABOR PRACTICE

The term used to describe labor practices forbidden by the National Labor Relations Act.

UNFAIR LABOR PRACTICE STRIKE

A strike caused or prolonged by an employer's unfair labor practices.

UNION CONSTITUTION

A book or document published by a union which contains the procedures and rules which bind union members.

UNION DUES

Monthly payments required from a union member to a union.

UNION SHOP

A company where employees represented by a union must join the union on or after the 30th day of their employment. If employees fail to join the union after the 30th day or thereafter fail to pay union dues and fees, the union may lawfully require the employer to discharge them.

TABLE OF CASES

A

B

J

K

L

M

U

V

W

Y

TOPICAL INDEX

246

L

Labor-Management Relations Act of 1947, As Amended (LMRA)
. employee rights . . . 3
. free speech . . . 91, 103-104
. supervisor's status—See also "Supervisors" . . . 101-102, 150-151
. unit for bargaining
.. bases for including or excluding employees—See also "Unit for Bargaining" . . . 147-148
.. Regional Director's determination of unit . . . 151

Labor-Management Reporting and Disclosure Act of 1959 (LMRDA)
. filing requirements . . . 82-83
. Forms LM-1 and LM-2 . . . 82-83
. Register of Reporting Organizations . . . 82

Landrum-Griffin Act—See "LMRDA"

Lawyer—See "Attorney"

Letters to Employees—See also "Campaigns; Organizing Techniques of Unions"
. communicating election results to employees . . . 224-225
. employer mailing to employees' homes . . . 168, 169, 171, 195-196
. fines and discipline by unions . . . 104, 105-106, 168
. strikes . . . 172
.. what unions can and cannot do . . . 106-107

Literature—See "Campaigns; Organizing Techniques of Unions"

M

Mail Ballot Elections—See "Elections"

Mailing—See "Campaigns; Elections; Organizing Techniques of Unions"

Mail Surveys—See also "Surveys" . . . 56

Majority Status—See "Recognition; Bargaining Orders"

Meetings, Employer-Employee—See also "Campaigns" . . . 33-34, 35-36, 88

Meetings, Organizational—See also "Organizing Techniques of Unions" . . . 63-64

Minority Union—See "Recognition; Bargaining Order"

Misrepresentations by Union—See "Campaigns; Organizing Techniques of Unions"

N

National Labor Relations Act . . . 3

National Labor Relations Board
. appointment of members . . . 3
. Certification of Results . . . 223, 227
. duties of the board . . . 3-4
. General Counsel . . . 4
. Notice of Designation of Representative as Agent for Service . . . 124, 136
. Notice to Employees . . . 124, 137
. organization by regions . . . 123
. petitions
.. filing and investigation—See also "Representation Petition" . . . 123, 125-126
. publications
.. Casehandling Manual . . . 4
.. Field Manual . . . 4
.. Rules and Regulations . . . 4
. structure . . . 3-4

Negotiation of Contract—See "Collective Bargaining Agreements"

No-Access Rule—See "Solicitation"

No-Distribution Rule—See "Solicitation"

No-Solicitation Rule—See "Solicitation"

Norris-Thermador Decision—See also "Representation Petition" . . . 143-144

Notice of Election—See also "Elections" . . . 195, 197, 199

Notice of Representation Hearing—See also "Representation Petition" . . . 124, 135

Notice to Employees—See also "Elections; Representation Petition" . . . 124, 137

Nursing Homes
. NLRB jurisdiction . . . 125

O

Objections to Election—See also "Elections"
. board review . . . 221-223
. conduct by pro-union supervisors . . . 219
. conduct by non-parties . . . 220
. contents of . . . 220
. examples of
.. union misconduct . . . 217-218
.. employer misconduct . . . 218
. exceptions . . . 222, 223
. investigation . . . 220-221
. propaganda . . . 217
. report on objections . . . 222
. right to hearing . . . 222, 223
. timeliness . . . 220

V

W